ACT IT OUT WITH
READERS' THEATER

Help students become fluent readers!

Grades 4–5

BY KATHRYN WHEELER

CARSON-DELLOSA PUBLISHING COMPANY, INC.
GREENSBORO, NORTH CAROLINA

CREDITS

Editor: Ashley Futrell
Layout Design: Jon Nawrocik
Inside Illustrations: Ray Lambert
Cover Design: Peggy Jackson
Cover Illustration: Dan Sharp

Printed in the USA • All rights reserved.   ISBN 1-59441-181-6

TABLE OF CONTENTS

INTRODUCTION

The advantages of readers' theater productions in the classroom are many. One of the strongest advantages is the evidence that readers' theater projects build reading fluency. The repeated readings necessary to prepare for a play, both silent and oral, help students gain confidence with the selected play text. Preliminary choral readings, rehearsals, and readings at home with family members all create great reading opportunities. Readers' theater also strengthens listening skills, allows for positive opportunities to practice speaking skills, builds confidence, and creates excitement and fun in the classroom. Children are natural actors, and even the shyest student can be a surprising performer when given the chance to have a part in a play. And, because actors in readers' theater productions read directly from their scripts, students are relieved of the stress of memorizing lines.

In this book, you will find plays that are connected to key curriculum areas. The teacher pages for each play offer background information along with a warm-up activity and curriculum connections. Every play has leveled parts so that readers of different abilities can be included. On the teacher's pages, you will find the roles of each play listed in four levels, with Level 1 Roles for struggling readers through Level 4 Roles for advanced readers. You can cast the play according to this guide and provide each student with a role that suits his reading skills.

Traditionally, readers' theater productions include very few, if any, props or costumes. However, the plays in this book can be used for full productions if you choose; each play includes suggestions for props, costumes, and staging. Finally, each play is followed by reproducible reading comprehension pages to use when checking students' understanding of content.

Within the pages of this book, you will find everything you need to make classroom performances as simple or elaborate as you wish. Either way, you'll be bringing reading fun and the joy of drama into the classroom!

PREPARING FOR PERFORMANCE

You will find a suggested warm-up activity on the first teacher's page of each play. However, you may also want to add elements of your own. For example, it is always a good idea to let students read the play silently before they begin performing it. Remember to introduce listed vocabulary words and discuss their definitions and pronunciations. You should then follow that with a choral reading. During the choral reading, try to make notes about other words that are causing difficulty. Then, follow the reading with a lesson about those words.

CASTING

You will have to decide how you want to cast each play. You may want to hold auditions, or you may choose to create several casts for the same play and perform it more than once. You might even decide to add parts to include more students. You can easily create parts for additional students by providing more group parts. For example, if the scene is a general store and the play calls for three clerks, add three more clerks that will read during the "All" lines. Because the plays provide leveled reading roles, you can add parts for certain students based on their reading abilities. If you need more parts for struggling readers, add more group lines. If you require more advanced-reader parts, divide the lines for an existing advanced part and create an additional character to share those lines. Or, if you enjoy writing drama, add an entirely new part to the play. The possibilities are endless!

REHEARSING AND DIRECTING

One great thing about readers' theater is the fact that it relieves the stress of memorization. The actors in readers' theater always have a copy of the script in hand, even during the final performance. However, you should make sure students understand that they need to be familiar with the play in order to act well. Reading the play multiple times helps increase familiarity. Suggest that students also take the play home and share it with their family members.

Readers' theater creates multiple opportunities for repeated readings because of rehearsals, but remember not to over-rehearse the cast. Students may grow tired of the play, and that can cause them to lose momentum. You are the best judge of the class's mood during the rehearsal period.

Suggest that students highlight their own parts to make them easier to read and follow during performances. Ask students to underline words that may give them pronunciation or emphasis difficulties.

Encourage creativity! Because the traditional readers' theater production is not "staged" with costumes, props, or set design, that only focuses more attention on the quality of the actual performance. Should a student try a different voice or a hand gesture to emphasize a line? What about facial expressions? Encourage students to really "act it out."

STAGING

There are several ways to stage a readers' theater production. One of the most common is having the actors stand in a row in front of the class. You may wish to borrow music stands to hold the scripts. This accomplishes two things. It gives students somewhere to place their scripts so that they can make hand gestures. And, it provides a "safety zone" for students, allowing them to stand behind things, which may make them feel more comfortable.

You can also have actors sit in a row of chairs. You may want each student to stand when it is her turn to deliver a line. Readers' theater productions can even be done with everyone sitting on the floor if that is more comfortable and fun.

ASSESSING

The Acting Review Rubric (page 8) can be used by you or the students. You can also evaluate students' skills by having them write paragraphs after the production to explain what they thought about the play and the performance.

EXPANDING READERS' THEATER

If you wish, any of the plays in this book can be used for full productions. On the teacher's pages for each play, you will find suggestions for costumes, props, and staging that you can create with students and adult volunteers. If you choose to perform a full production, you can assign students who are not actors to work as the director, stage managers, and set and costume designers. You can also assign understudies so that more students will be able to practice their reading and acting skills during the rehearsal phase of the play.

ACT WELL YOUR PART

Review this checklist of ideas as you prepare for the performance.

GETTING READY

- Be sure to mark your part in the play. Use a highlighting marker.
- Read the play and think about your character. What is the character like?
- Say aloud the words that give you trouble. Make sure you know what they mean.
- Read the play with your family or friends. Talk about it with them.
- Read the play at least four times. It will help you perform better.

PRACTICING

- Talk slowly and clearly. Don't get nervous and talk too fast.
- Speak loudly. Make sure students in the back of the room can hear you.
- Talk with lots of feeling. Make sure others understand your character's personality.
- Think of the way that your character talks. Use your hands to make gestures for emphasis.
- Practice your part at home in front of a mirror. Watch your face as you speak your part.
- When it is not your turn to speak, stand or sit still. Pay attention to the play.
- Sit or stand up straight. It will help you speak clearly and loudly.
- When you practice with the rest of the cast, be nice to the other actors and help them with good ideas. Work as a team!

ACTING

- Take a few deep breaths before the play begins. It will help to keep you calm.
- If someone makes a mistake, pretend not to notice.
- If you make a mistake, keep going!
- If someone talks or moves in the room, don't look at the person.
- If you drop your script, pick it up after you finish the line you are speaking, unless you can't remember it.
- Remember all of the things you practiced and have fun during the play!

Act It Out with Readers' Theater • Grades 4-5

ACTING REVIEW RUBRIC

Actor's Name: _____

Name of Play: _____

	ALWAYS	**MOST OF THE TIME**	**SOMETIMES**
READ LOUDLY I could hear this actor easily.			
READ SLOWLY AND CLEARLY I could understand this actor's words.			
READ WITH FEELING I believed this character's words.			
LOOKED UP FROM THE SCRIPT I could see this actor's face.			
STOOD OR SAT STILL This actor listened to and responded to other actors in the play.			

REWIND

BACKGROUND

"Rewind" is a character education play. It reminds students to choose their words and actions carefully to avoid unpleasant outcomes. The play also emphasizes making responsible choices. Three different scenes show students that a change in attitude and words can create a completely different and more pleasant ending to each scenario.

WARM-UP ACTIVITY

Read Carl Sandburg's 1922 poem, "Primer Lesson." This poem warns the reader to be careful when he uses "proud words" and goes on to explain that once you say something regrettable, it is not easy to retract or correct the situation. The poem can be found on-line or in collections of Sandburg's work. Use "Primer Lesson" to spark a discussion about saying or doing things that cause conflict with others. Next, introduce the play and distribute copies of the script. Ask students to read it on their own first. You can encourage repeat readings by having "auditions" for various parts, or you can assign parts based on students' reading levels.

CASTING

The parts in the play are written for readers of different levels, from Level 1 Roles (struggling readers) to Level 4 Roles (advanced readers).

LEVEL 4 ROLES
Narrator   Advisor #3

LEVEL 3 ROLES
Advisor #1   Dad   Nikki
Ms. Olivarez   Mr. Ruello

LEVEL 2 ROLES
Advisor #2   Juanita   Jason
Brian

LEVEL 1 ROLES
Sound Effects Person   Becky

DISCUSSION

- What does it mean to rewind something? Have you ever rewound a movie to watch a scene again? Why did you want to watch it again?
- Have you ever wished that you could go back and say or do something differently?
- Think about a time when you wish you had thought more before speaking or you did something that you regretted later. What could you have done differently in that situation?

VOCABULARY TO REVIEW

advisor   scene   actually   diorama   rewind

WRITING CONNECTION

Give students a scene from a story or from real life that they can "rewind," using the examples in the play as a model. Have them write dialogue for the new scene. Then, ask students to add narration to make the story flow into a work of fiction.

SOCIAL STUDIES CONNECTION

Can you think of a time in history that people might like to rewind and redo? Choose an event or period from history and talk about how things might have changed if just one thing had occurred differently, or if one person had not done something that triggered a series of events.

COSTUME, PROP, AND SET DESIGN SUGGESTIONS

COSTUMES: *Sound Effects Person*–completely in black; *Advisors*–all three should be dressed alike in white; *Ms. Olivarez*–dress or skirt and top, glasses; *Mr. Ruello* and *Dad*–dress shirt and pants; *Students*–school clothes; *Children (when not at school)*–age-appropriate outfits; *Narrator*–dress or suit

PROPS: Backpacks and books for first scene; "cheat sheet" for Jason's sleeve, pencil and paper for his desk; baseball gloves and baseball; remote control and piece of paper for advisors

SET DESIGN: Three chairs and table for advisors to sit beside the action; student desk and chair for Jason's scene; backdrops of a school hallway, a classroom, and a backyard

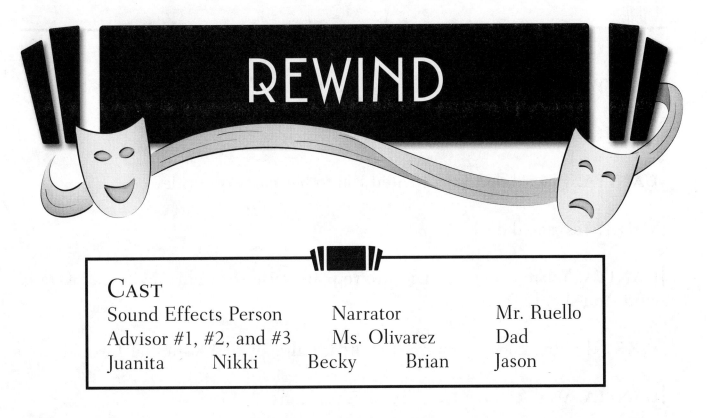

REWIND

CAST

Sound Effects Person	Narrator	Mr. Ruello
Advisor #1, #2, and #3	Ms. Olivarez	Dad
Juanita Nikki	Becky Brian	Jason

SETTING: *A large, white room. The narrator stands in one corner. Three advisors dressed in white sit behind a long, white table. There is a huge video screen. Playing on the screen is a scene in a school hallway.*

JUANITA: You're not my friend anymore! You were never my friend!

NIKKI: Well, you're not my friend either. Don't talk to me again!

NARRATOR: Nikki and Juanita have been best friends since first grade. You wouldn't know that from looking at this tape, would you?

ADVISOR #1: No, you would not.

ADVISOR #2: How did this bad fight happen?

ADVISOR #3: Let's rewind to the beginning and find out.

SOUND EFFECTS PERSON: *(sound of tape rewinding)* Whiiiiiirr! Ding!

NARRATOR: Here's the scene from the beginning.

JUANITA: Nikki! Wait up! I need to talk to you.

NIKKI: Hi, Juanita. What's up?

JUANITA: I heard that Kara invited you to her party on Friday.

NIKKI: Yes, she did.

JUANITA: You're not going to go, are you? Because she didn't invite me! Kara is awful. You shouldn't go.

NIKKI: I didn't know you weren't invited. I already told Kara that I would go.

JUANITA: Well, call her back! Tell her you can't.

NIKKI: No, I can't do that. I have to go now.

JUANITA: How can you do this to me? It isn't fair!

NIKKI: It's not fair of you to ask me not to go. I can't help it that Kara doesn't like you.

JUANITA: (shouting) If you're friends with her, you can't be friends with me!

NIKKI: (angry) Why are you acting like this?

JUANITA: You're not my friend anymore! You were never my friend!

NIKKI: Well, you're not my friend either. Don't talk to me again!

NARRATOR: Well? What do you think?

ADVISOR #2: We can fix this.

ADVISOR #1: Nikki needs to ask Juanita if she was invited, too.

ADVISOR #3: And, Juanita needs to be honest about her feelings. She needs to understand that Nikki is still her friend. OK, rewind!

SOUND EFFECTS PERSON: *(sound of tape rewinding)* Whiiiiiirr! Ding!

NIKKI: Hi, Juanita. What's up?

JUANITA: I heard that Kara invited you to her party on Friday.

NIKKI: Yes, she did. Did she invite you, too?

JUANITA: No, she didn't. I feel really sad about it.

NIKKI: I didn't know you weren't invited. I'm sorry. That was kind of mean of Kara to do that.

JUANITA: Can you tell her you won't go?

NIKKI: I already told Kara I would go. If I had known she left you out, I might not have said yes. But listen, we can do something together on Saturday. OK?

JUANITA: You're still my friend?

NIKKI: Of course I am. Are you still my friend?

JUANITA: Yes!

NARRATOR: OK, that wasn't so hard. It's better to be honest about feelings. Let's look at another tape. This one is from Ms. Olivarez's classroom.

MS. OLIVAREZ: Jason, would you come up here, please?

JASON: What do you want?

MS. OLIVAREZ: I think you know what I want. You were just cheating on the test. I saw you.

JASON: *(angrily)* I was not!

MS. OLIVAREZ: Jason, what's that paper up your sleeve?

NARRATOR: This looks bad for Jason. And you know what? He's actually a very good student.

ADVISOR #1: Let's rewind this one.

ADVISOR #2: I have a note here that says we should rewind the tape all the way to this morning.

ADVISOR #3: Let's run that tape, please.

SOUND EFFECTS PERSON: *(sound of tape rewinding)* Whiiiiiirr! Ding!

DAD: Jason, don't you have a social studies test today?

JASON: Yes, Dad.

DAD: Well, I hope you're ready for it. You haven't been doing so well in social studies lately. I'm worried about your grade.

JASON: I studied for hours.

DAD: Well, just do your best, son. I know you want to pull up that grade.

NARRATOR: Jason doesn't want to let his dad down.

ADVISOR #1: But, he knows he has a lot of trouble in social studies.

ADVISOR #3: If Jason gets caught cheating, his dad will be even more let down. Instead of planning to cheat, Jason needs to talk to Ms. Olivarez. She can help him make a plan.

ADVISOR #2: We can fix this one! Let's rewind!

SOUND EFFECTS PERSON: *(sound of tape rewinding)* Whiiiiiirr! Ding!

JASON: Ms. Olivarez, can I talk to you for a minute before we start the test?

MS. OLIVAREZ: Of course, Jason. What is it?

JASON: I'm really worried about the social studies test today. I studied hard. But, I can't remember the dates and places.

MS. OLIVAREZ: I have noticed that. What do you like about social studies?

JASON: Some of the stories are really cool.

MS. OLIVAREZ: You made a great diorama for our Civil War study.

JASON: That was fun! When I was making it, it was like I could see what really happened during the battle.

MS. OLIVAREZ: OK. I'll tell you what. You do your best on this test today. But, if you don't do well, I will let you make another diorama for extra credit.

JASON: Really? That's great! Thanks, Ms. Olivarez.

NARRATOR: That worked out well. Now, let's look at something that happened in Brian's backyard. He and his sister Becky were playing catch after school.

BECKY: Brian, you threw that one too high for me!

SOUND EFFECTS PERSON: (sound of ball hitting glass) CRASH!!!

BRIAN: Oh, no! I broke Mr. Ruello's window!

BECKY: Run, Brian!

BRIAN: No, Becky! Wait!

MR. RUELLO: (angrily) Brian! Did you throw that ball at my house?

BRIAN: No, I didn't . . . I mean . . . well . . . I . . .

MR. RUELLO: Are you lying to me?

BRIAN: (scared) No, I'm not lying! I didn't throw the ball at your house. I . . .

MR. RUELLO: Then, who broke my window? Whose ball is this?

BRIAN: That is my ball, but I . . .

MR. RUELLO: *(sternly)* Brian, you're the only one out here. You said this is your ball. I don't think you're telling me the truth. I will need to speak to your parents about this.

NARRATOR: Well, advisors? What do you think?

ADVISOR #2: We can fix this! This one isn't hard at all.

ADVISOR #1: Brian is trying to tell Mr. Ruello the truth, but he's too scared.

ADVISOR #3: And, because he's looking down at the ground and not finishing his sentences, he looks like he's lying. He needs to try to stay calm. OK, rewind!

SOUND EFFECTS PERSON: *(sound of tape rewinding)* Whiiiiiirr! Ding!

MR. RUELLO: *(angrily)* Brian! Did you throw that ball at my house?

BRIAN: I didn't mean to throw the ball at your house. I threw it too high. It went over the fence.

MR. RUELLO: So, it was an accident?

BRIAN: Yes, Mr. Ruello. I'm really sorry.

MR. RUELLO: It's OK. Accidents happen. Thanks for telling me the truth, Brian. Let's go talk to your parents about working out a plan to pay for the window. I'm sure you can do some extra chores to earn the money.

NARRATOR: Sometimes it's hard to know what to do when things go wrong. Whether you accidentally break a window . . .

SOUND EFFECTS PERSON: *(sound of ball hitting glass)* CRASH!!!

NARRATOR: . . . or get nervous . . .

SOUND EFFECTS PERSON: *(sound of mumbling and pacing back and forth)* What if . . . but then . . . no, I . . . I could . . . Well, then . . . Oh, no . . . I just don't know . . .

NARRATOR: . . . or get angry with someone . . .

SOUND EFFECTS PERSON: *(sound of door slamming)* SLAM!!!

NARRATOR: . . . just take a deep breath, take your time, and think about what you will say or do. Because then you won't need to rewind!

18

COMPREHENSION QUESTIONS

Circle your answer.

1. Who is having a party?

    a. Nikki

    b. Becky

    c. Juanita

    d. Kara

2. Whose window gets broken?

    a. Ms. Olivarez

    b. Dad

    c. Mr. Ruello

    d. Jason

3. What is the moral of this play?

    a. Think before you speak.

    b. You can always rewind and fix a mistake.

    c. Be careful not to ruin a friendship.

    d. A penny saved is a penny earned.

Write a short answer.

4. Why did Jason cheat on his test before his scene was rewound?

    _____

    _____

    _____

    _____

5. Why wasn't Brian able to tell Mr. Ruello the truth about the window before his scene was rewound?

    _____

    _____

    _____

6. Was Juanita really angry at Nikki? Explain.

    _____

    _____

    _____

Act It Out with Readers' Theater • Grades 4-5

COMPREHENSION QUESTIONS

Imagine you are a helper in a kindergarten classroom. You look out the window at recess and see the scene below. Circle three students or groups of students that you feel you should talk to about their words or actions. What advice would you give them? Write your advice on the lines below.

1. _____

2. _____

3. _____

Circle your answers.

4. Read the list of rules below. As a teacher's helper, which three rules do you think are the most important things for young children to learn about how to treat others?

Don't start fights.   Don't push other people.   Don't yell.   Have fun.

Don't call people names.   Be kind to each other.   Listen carefully.   Be fair.

Write a short answer.

5. Why did you choose these three rules?

_____

_____

SYNONYM OLYMPICS

Language Arts

BACKGROUND

"Synonym Olympics" is a language arts play. Use it to emphasize the study of synonyms and antonyms. Reintroduce and demonstrate how to use synonyms and antonyms before students begin rehearsing and reading this play. This can also be a fun play to actually perform because it requires limited action and set design for a full production. You can easily add nonspeaking parts for judges and more spectators so that you can include more students in the performance.

WARM-UP ACTIVITY

Show a recording of an Olympic event that includes the ratings of judges from various countries. Figure skating and gymnastics are good choices because the individual performances are short, and the judges' scores are available immediately after the performance. Discuss the method of judging and ranking the athletes. Next, introduce the play and distribute copies of the script. Ask students to read it on their own first. You can encourage repeat readings by having "auditions" for various parts, or you can assign parts based on students' reading levels.

CASTING

The parts in the play are written for readers of different levels, from Level 1 Roles (struggling readers) to Level 4 Roles (advanced readers). To include more students in the performance, have five students sit at a table and play nonspeaking judges who display scorecards.

LEVEL 4 ROLES
Announcer #1 (Beth) and #2 (Sam)

LEVEL 3 ROLES
Myra Moon   Steve Abdul

LEVEL 2 ROLES
Ty Jackson   Chang Lee
Justin Riggs   Jennie Camilla

LEVEL 1 ROLES
4 spectators   5 judges (nonspeaking)

DISCUSSION

- Have you ever watched the Olympic games? What is your favorite event?
- Can you think of any language events that occur competitively with judging? (speeches, debates, spelling bees, etc.) Have you ever played a part in these types of events?
- What would it feel like to compete in an event like the one in the play? Would it be easy or hard? Why do you think so?

VOCABULARY TO REVIEW

spectator	announcer	competition	synonym
antonym	partial	veteran (experienced)	endeavor
opposite	minute (small)	impolite	triathlon

ART CONNECTION

Ask students to make collages using pictures that represent opposites. Call it "Antonym Art." Ask students to give short presentations about their collages and explain all of the antonyms that are represented in the pictures.

SCIENCE CONNECTION

Science is full of related terms and terms of opposition. Have students read a science selection or experiment and find all of the "synonyms" and "antonyms" in the text.

COSTUME, PROP, AND SET DESIGN SUGGESTIONS

COSTUMES: *Students*–regular school clothes (or uniforms if students at your school wear them); *Announcers*–dress and suit; *Judges*–dresses and suits with sashes that say "Judge" on them; *Spectators*–regular casual clothes

PROPS: Borrow headphones for announcers from media center; microphones for announcers: cut a large foam ball in half, place the cut side down, insert a dowel diagonally into the ball, insert a foam rectangle onto the other end of the dowel, and spray paint black; two gold medals and one silver medal (available at party stores); preprogrammed scorecards, pencils, and paper for judges

SET DESIGN: Chairs or portable risers arranged in a semicircle to represent stadium seating; table and chairs for judges; table with floor-length tablecloth for announcer booth; student-made poster for front of table that reads "WGRM Grammar Radio;" six chairs for contestants

SYNONYM OLYMPICS

CAST

Announcer #1 (Beth)   Announcer #2 (Sam)
Ty Jackson   Chang Lee   Justin Riggs
Jennie Camilla   Steve Abdul   Myra Moon
Spectator #1, #2, #3, and #4   five judges (nonspeaking)

SETTING: *An auditorium filled with spectators. Five judges sit behind a long, low table and the two announcers are in a press booth. The crowd is buzzing with excitement.*

ANNOUNCER #1: Well, here we are, at the opening day of the Synonym Olympics. You've seen the athletes, Sam. Who do you think is going to take home the gold medal?

ANNOUNCER #2: Beth, it's going to be a close one today. Our returning champion, Myra Moon, has been practicing for months. But, she has strong competition in Steve Abdul and Jennie Camilla.

ANNOUNCER #1: Plus, we have some newcomers: Ty Jackson, Chang Lee, and Justin Riggs. What do you think about them, Sam?

ANNOUNCER #2: Beth, any of them could cause an upset here today. Usually, newcomers struggle in the antonym round. Experience pays off then. We'll just have to see what happens today.

ANNOUNCER #1: You're right. Let's see what happens. Here's our first contender. It's Ty Jackson!

SPECTATOR #1: Go, Ty!

ANNOUNCER #2: Here's the first word up on the screen. It looks like a noun . . . yes, the word is "rocks."

TY JACKSON: *(calling out)* Stones!

ANNOUNCER #1: Well done. And here's the second word . . . it's "woods."

TY JACKSON: *(calling out)* Forest!

ANNOUNCER #2: That's a perfect score so far, Beth. But, here comes something a little more challenging. It's a verb . . . "snooze."

TY JACKSON: Um, Uh . . . sneeze?

(Judges confer, and Judge #1 holds up a 5.5 scorecard.)

ANNOUNCER #1: Ouch! The judges are showing Ty Jackson's overall score as a 5.5. That last round cost him, Sam.

ANNOUNCER #2: It sure did, Beth. Here's the next contestant. It's Chang Lee. Now, Beth, you remember that we talked about the antonym round. First, let's see if Chang can hold up for the three synonym rounds.

SPECTATOR #2: You show 'em, Chang!

ANNOUNCER #1: And the first word is . . . "glad."

CHANG LEE: *(calling out)* Happy!

ANNOUNCER #2: That was a pretty easy one, Beth. Here comes the second word . . . it's "huge."

CHANG LEE: (*calling out*) Large!

ANNOUNCER #1: Ooh . . . it looks like the judges are only going to give partial credit for that one, Sam.

ANNOUNCER #2: Yes, I agree. While "large" is a synonym for "huge," I think Chang would have done better if he had gone with "enormous" or "gigantic."

SPECTATOR #3: Come on, Chang! Concentrate!

ANNOUNCER #1: Chang is still in the running though. Here's the third word . . . it's a verb, "trail."

CHANG LEE: (*calling out*) Path!

ANNOUNCER #2: Oh, no! Chang didn't notice that it was a verb! He gave a synonym for "trail" as a noun. And Chang Lee is OUT.

SPECTATOR #2: Too bad, Chang!

ANNOUNCER #1: That's right, Sam. If the word "trail" had been a noun, then "path" would have been a good synonym. But, "trail" as a verb means "follow."

(Judges confer, and Judge #2 holds up a 4.1 scorecard.)

ANNOUNCER #2: And Chang Lee ends up with a total score of only 4.1. Next up: Justin Riggs.

SPECTATOR #4: *(cheering)* Yay, Justin! Go, Justin!

ANNOUNCER #1: And Justin's first word is . . . "toss."

JUSTIN RIGGS: *(calling out)* Throw!

ANNOUNCER #2: Yes, it looks like the judges are going to accept that answer. Next word . . . "destroy."

JUSTIN RIGGS: Um . . . destruction?

ANNOUNCER #1: Oh, no! I thought that Justin looked too nervous when he came out onto the floor, Sam.

ANNOUNCER #2: Yes, Beth. That was an unfortunate mistake. He had a verb and just gave the noun for the word, not a synonym. Justin Riggs is OUT.

SPECTATOR #4: Justin! Good try!

ANNOUNCER #1: Considering that this is Justin's first Olympics, it was a good try. Now, we're going to see returning veteran Jennie Camilla at work.

ANNOUNCER #2: Jennie's had some great training, Beth. Here's her first word . . . "endeavor."

JENNIE CAMILLA: *(calling out)* Try!

ANNOUNCER #1: Great job! That was a tough word. Here comes her second word. It's . . . "tear," a verb.

JENNIE CAMILLA: *(calling out)* Rip!

ANNOUNCER #2: Excellent. She's fast, she's calm, and she's concentrating. Third word . . . a noun, "answer."

JENNIE CAMILLA: *(calling out)* Solution!

ANNOUNCER #1: *(tense)* OK. Now, she has to be on her toes. Here comes the antonym round. That means her next answer has to be the opposite of the word she's given. And the word is . . . "shout."

JENNIE CAMILLA: *(calling out)* Yell!

SPECTATOR #1: Oh, no, Jennie! Too bad!

ANNOUNCER #2: Jennie clearly forgot she was switching from synonyms to antonyms, Beth.

(Judges confer, and Judge #3 holds up an 8.2 scorecard.)

ANNOUNCER #1: Yes, Sam, you're right. But, the judges are giving her an 8.2. She did do some great synonym work out there. Our next contestant is silver medalist Steve Abdul.

ANNOUNCER #2: Steve's words are bound to be challenging. Let's take a look. The first word is . . . "create."

STEVE ABDUL: *(calling out)* Invent!

ANNOUNCER #1: The next word is . . . "brilliant."

STEVE ABDUL: *(calling out)* Intelligent!

SPECTATOR #2: Way to go, Steve!

ANNOUNCER #2: That was a good answer. It was a better choice than "smart," although "smart" would have been correct, too. The next word is a verb: "exit."

STEVE ABDUL: *(calling out)* Leave!

ANNOUNCER #1: OK, now we're going to the antonym round. Remember, Steve's next answer has to be the opposite of the word he's given. And . . . I don't believe this, Sam! The judges are giving Steve the noun "exit!"

SPECTATOR #3: Careful, Steve!

SPECTATOR #4: Take your time!

STEVE ABDUL: *(calling out)* Entrance!

(Judges confer, and Judge #4 holds up a 9.6 scorecard.)

ANNOUNCER #2: Wow! What a champion! That was a very hard round. And, the judges are giving him a score of 9.6!

ANNOUNCER #1: *(excited)* Sam, this is clearly the person who could take the gold medal away from Myra Moon. And, here comes Myra now. She looks ready for the challenge. Her first word is . . . "mend."

MYRA MOON: *(calling out)* Repair!

SPECTATOR #1: Go, Myra!

ANNOUNCER #2: OK. Here's the second word . . . it's "tiny."

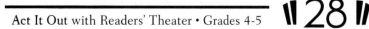

MYRA MOON: *(calling out)* Minute!

ANNOUNCER #1: Here's what separates the champions from the beginners, Sam. Myra could have said "small" or "little," but she chose a much more difficult synonym. The judges are giving her full marks.

ANNOUNCER #2: And, her third word is coming up now. It looks like it's going to be an adjective: "rude."

MYRA MOON: *(calling out)* Impolite!

SPECTATOR #3: Great job, Myra!

SPECTATOR #2: You're the best, Myra!

ANNOUNCER #1: And now we're in the antonym round of this close, close contest, Sam . . . and the word is . . . "damp."

MYRA MOON: *(calling out)* Dry!

ANNOUNCER #2: *(thoughtful)* The scoring should be interesting here, Beth. Myra's round was a little easier than Steve's.

(Judges confer, and Judge #5 holds up a 9.6 scorecard.)

ANNOUNCER #1: But still, Myra gave us some great synonyms and a perfectly correct antonym, Sam. Let's see . . . I don't believe it!

SPECTATOR #3: It's a tie!

SPECTATOR #4: Hooray for Myra!

SPECTATOR #1: Hooray for Steve!

SPECTATOR #2: A tie?

ANNOUNCER #1: Yes, it's a tie! Myra Moon and Steve Abdul will share the gold medal for the synonym event. That means that Jennie Camilla will take home the silver.

ANNOUNCER #2: This is a historic moment, Beth. The champions are coming out now to receive their medals.

SPECTATORS: (all cheering) Hooray!

ANNOUNCER #1: This is the end of tonight's broadcast from the Synonym Olympics. Tomorrow night, we'll see some more language challenges in the Adverb Advantage trials.

ANNOUNCER #2: And, stay tuned on Friday to see the grammar giants compete in a fascinating contest of wits: the Complex Sentence Triathlon.

ANNOUNCER #1: Good night from the Synonym Olympics, and remember, language arts is awesome!

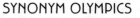
COMPREHENSION QUESTIONS

Circle your answer.

1. What is a *competition*?

   a. an adventure

   b. a contest

   c. a lesson

   d. a communication

2. What is an *endeavor*?

   a. an attempt

   b. a kind of vegetable

   c. a failure

   d. an endowment

3. Who was the silver medalist in the synonym event?

   a. Ty Jackson

   b. Myra Moon

   c. Jennie Camilla

   d. Steve Abdul

Write a synonym for each word.

4. beautiful

   _____

5. worried

   _____

6. powerful

   _____

7. hot

   _____

8. scholar

   _____

Write an antonym for each word.

9. dull

   _____

10. dark

    _____

11. tragic

    _____

12. sunny

    _____

13. swift

    _____

COMPREHENSION QUESTIONS

Imagine that your class is going to perform "Synonym Olympics." You will be the director. Fill out the director's plan to show your ideas for the play.

1. In addition to the characters that are already listed, what other parts would you add?

   _____

   _____

2. Describe the costumes for the following characters:

   the athletes _____

   the announcers _____

   the spectators _____

   the judges _____

3. Describe what the set will look like. Remember that you have to plan the set so that the audience can see everything that is going on.

   _____

   _____

4. List at least six props that you will need for the play. (For example, you will need scorecards for the judges.)

   _____

   _____

   _____

5. What sound effects will you want for the play? List at least three different sounds you will need.

   _____

   _____

PLAY BALL, CINDERELLA

Language Arts

BACKGROUND

"Play Ball, Cinderella" is based on a well-known fairy tale. There are many versions of the Cinderella fairy tale, extending across many cultures. The version that most people know best is originally from France. Charles Perrault, a French lawyer who lived from 1628 to 1703, first recorded the story, but it is not known if he was familiar with earlier oral versions of the tale. Perrault's most famous works include "Little Red Riding Hood," "Puss in Boots," and "Tales of Mother Goose." The version of "Cinderella" found in this play is known as a "fractured fairy tale"—one that is modernized and humorous, with twists and turns that are not in the original story.

WARM-UP ACTIVITY

Read aloud Perrault's traditional version of "Cinderella." Discuss it with the class. Next, introduce the play and distribute copies of the script. Ask students to read it on their own first. As a group, compare and contrast the two versions. Is the original tale funny? Which characters are different? How do the stories end? Guide students to see that fractured fairy tales are parodies—they're meant to be funny because they vary so much from the original tale. Encourage students to choose another fairy tale, read it in its traditional version, then discuss ways to "fracture" the story.

CASTING

The parts in the play are written for readers of different levels, from Level 1 Roles (struggling readers) to Level 4 Roles (advanced readers).

LEVEL 4 ROLE
Narrator #2

LEVEL 3 ROLES
Cinderella	Stepmother
Fairy Godfather	Brendan

LEVEL 2 ROLES
Narrator #1	Latisha

LEVEL 1 ROLES
Mia	Janet	Paulo

Act It Out with Readers' Theater • Grades 4-5

DISCUSSION

- Have you ever wanted to do something that your family didn't want you to do? What was it?
- What are your goals for your life? What do you want to do when you are older?
- What versions of "Cinderella" have you read or heard before? Tell the class about another version of the story.

VOCABULARY TO REVIEW

frilly	ruffles	patent leather	cleats
outfielder	ladylike	limped	forfeit

SOCIAL STUDIES CONNECTION

Find a version of "Yeh-Shen" on-line or at the library. This is the Chinese version of Cinderella, and it is probably the oldest known version of the tale. Have students read the story. Then, discuss the elements of the story that are different from Perrault's version because of the cultural differences between Europe and Asia.

ART CONNECTION

Ask students to draw costume designs for the characters of "Play Ball, Cinderella" and contrast them with designs for the original characters. You can assign one character to each student and ask students to create designs for both the original and the fractured fairy tale versions of the characters.

COSTUME, PROP, AND SET DESIGN SUGGESTIONS

COSTUMES: *Narrators*–suits or dresses; *Cinderella*–first outfit: slouchy jeans and T-shirt, barefoot; second outfit: white frilly dress, black patent-leather shoes; third outfit: baseball cap, baseball jersey, cleats; fourth outfit: ripped, frilly white dress with dirt stains; hair in ponytail for all; *Stepsisters* and *Stepmother*–dresses, bows in hair, very prissy; *Baseball players*–matching baseball uniforms; *Fairy Godfather*–suit, make a tie from a strip of glittery or shiny material

PROPS: Book for Cinderella to read at the beginning; white glove; canned pumpkin; orange bicycle (or red if can't find orange); baseball bat and gloves

SET DESIGN: Kitchen table and chairs for the scenes at Cinderella's home; wooden bench to represent a dugout for baseball scenes

PLAY BALL, CINDERELLA

CAST
Cinderella   Stepmother   Fairy Godfather
Paulo   Latisha   Narrator #1 and #2
Brendan   Janet and Mia (stepsisters)

SETTING: *The play begins at Cinderella's house, a fancy two-story home with a beautiful flower garden. Later, the setting changes to a baseball diamond.*

NARRATOR #1: Cinderella was one lucky girl . . . or so everyone thought.

NARRATOR #2: She lived in a nice house. She had a stepmother who loved her. She had two really nice stepsisters. But was Cinderella happy?

CINDERELLA: No, I am not.

NARRATOR #2: You see, Cinderella's stepmother wanted her to be what she called "a little lady." And Cinderella thought all of that lace and frills stuff was bad news.

STEPMOTHER: Cinderella! I have such a surprise for you, darling!

JANET: Just wait until you see it!

MIA: You'll love it!

CINDERELLA: Somehow, I doubt it.

STEPMOTHER: Look, darling! I bought you a new dress for the ball that your dance class is having today. Isn't it beautiful? You will have to be very careful since it is white. Look at all of these ruffles!

MIA: Show her the shoes!

STEPMOTHER: Oh, just look at these cute patent-leather shoes, Cinderella!

CINDERELLA: Ick.

JANET: Please don't say that!

MIA: We shopped all morning for these.

CINDERELLA: Please don't make me wear this! I will look like a lamp shade.

❚❚36❚❚

STEPMOTHER: Just try it on, darling.

NARRATOR #1: So, Cinderella tried on the big, frilly, white dress and the very shiny shoes.

NARRATOR #2: And she looked just like a lamp shade.

CINDERELLA: (unhappily) You just can't make me wear this! Please don't make me go to the ball!

JANET: But, Cinderella! Mia and I have been waiting all year for this.

MIA: Please go with us. We want you to have fun!

STEPMOTHER: Now, girls. If Cinderella really doesn't want to go with us, she doesn't have to. We don't want her to be unhappy.

CINDERELLA: But, I am unhappy.

NARRATOR #1: Cinderella's stepmother and her stepsisters got into their fancy dresses and their shiny shoes. They left for the ball.

NARRATOR #2: And Cinderella sat on the edge of her bed in her frilly white dress and thought about how unhappy she was.

FAIRY GODFATHER: Why are you so unhappy, Cinderella?

CINDERELLA: (surprised) Who are you?

FAIRY GODFATHER: I'm your fairy godfather. I've been watching over you for years. And I want to fix things in your life, but first you have to tell me how.

CINDERELLA: I don't want to go to balls! I want to go to ball GAMES!

Act It Out with Readers' Theater • Grades 4-5

FAIRY GODFATHER: To watch or to play?

CINDERELLA: To play! I can hit a ball out of the park, and I'm a great left fielder. But, my stepmother says it's not ladylike to play baseball.

FAIRY GODFATHER: Is there a game today?

CINDERELLA: Yes, but I can't go to it.

FAIRY GODFATHER: Why not?

CINDERELLA: I don't have a uniform. I don't have a glove. I don't have cleats. And, I don't have any way to get to the field.

FAIRY GODFATHER: (thinking) Hmmm . . . I think we can do something about that. I'm going to need a glove and a pumpkin.

CINDERELLA: Here's a lacy glove that matches this lamp shade dress. And there's canned pumpkin down in the kitchen. Will that be good enough?

FAIRY GODFATHER: Excellent.

NARRATOR #1: The fairy godfather waved his hands. Sparks flew around Cinderella's dress, faster and faster.

NARRATOR #2: Her dress became a brand new baseball uniform. The white, lacy glove turned into a baseball glove. And on her feet were two black, patent-leather cleats.

FAIRY GODFATHER: Um . . . sorry about the shoes. Patent leather is really hard to change.

CINDERELLA: That's OK! What happened to the pumpkin?

FAIRY GODFATHER: Go downstairs and take a look.

NARRATOR #1: So, Cinderella ran down the stairs.

NARRATOR #2: And there, by the kitchen door, was a brand new, bright orange mountain bike.

CINDERELLA: Awesome!

FAIRY GODFATHER: I thought you'd like it. Now, what time will your stepmother and stepsisters be home?

CINDERELLA: At five thirty.

FAIRY GODFATHER: Then, you have to be done playing baseball and be back home at five o'clock. You don't want to worry your stepmother. Everything will change back at five. Got it?

CINDERELLA: Got it!

NARRATOR #1: Off Cinderella rode to the baseball diamond.

BRENDAN: This is a disaster! Jeremy broke his leg. He'll be out for the rest of the season. We're one player short. We may have to forfeit.

PAULO: What can we do?

LATISHA: Look! Here comes someone.

CINDERELLA: I'm ready to play if you want me to.

BRENDAN: We don't have a choice. Can you play left field?

CINDERELLA: (smiling) Yes, I can!

NARRATOR #1: The game started. And what a game it was!

NARRATOR #2: Cinderella caught fly balls. She threw out three runners at home plate. Her team was ahead when she was up to bat.

BRENDAN: If you can hit like you can field, we'll be in great shape.

CINDERELLA: I can hit. Don't worry.

LATISHA: Look at that! She hit the first pitch over the center fielder's head!

BRENDAN: Run! Run! Go, Cinderella, go!

NARRATOR #1: Cinderella started to run.

NARRATOR #2: She ran to first base . . . and then to second base . . . and then to third base.

PAULO: (calling) Stay there!

CINDERELLA: No, I can make it!

NARRATOR #1: Just as the outfielder threw the ball to the catcher . . .

NARRATOR #2: . . . Cinderella slid into home plate.

LATISHA: It's a home run!

BRENDAN: That was amazing. Wait, why are you running away? Where are you going? Wait! Stop!

CINDERELLA: It's five o'clock! I have to go home now!

BRENDAN: Wait! Here's one of your cleats. It fell off your foot!

LATISHA: (*blinking*) Uh . . . was she wearing a dress?

PAULO: A white dress?

NARRATOR #1: Yes, Cinderella's uniform had turned back into her dress.

NARRATOR #2: Her mountain bike had become canned pumpkin again. And, she had lost one of her shoes. She limped all the way home and found her stepmother and stepsisters nervously waiting for her.

STEPMOTHER: Oh, Cinderella! What happened to your dress? It's all dirty! And look, you've lost one of your shoes.

CINDERELLA: I had to slide into home. Um . . . I mean, I had a hard time getting home.

JANET: Poor Cinderella!

MIA: Let me clean your dress for you.

CINDERELLA: *(tired)* That's okay, Mia. But thanks anyway.

STEPMOTHER: That's the doorbell. Who could it be?

BRENDAN: Hi. I'm looking for the girl who owns this shoe.

STEPMOTHER: I have three daughters. But none of them own anything that looks like that. What a weird looking shoe. What's it for?

BRENDAN: It's a baseball cleat. Are you sure you don't know who owns it? It's really important that I find her.

CINDERELLA: Hi, Brendan. That's my shoe. See?

NARRATOR #1: Cinderella put on the cleat.

BRENDAN: (smiling) It fits perfectly! Will you be our new left fielder? The team really needs you.

CINDERELLA: (to her stepmother) May I please? I promise I'll keep going to dance classes if you let me play baseball.

STEPMOTHER: What do you think, Janet and Mia?

JANET AND MIA: (singing) "Take me out to the ball game!"

CINDERELLA: (laughing) Thanks, you two!

BRENDAN: Practice is every Thursday at four o'clock. See you there.

CINDERELLA: (softly) Thanks, Fairy Godfather!

FAIRY GODFATHER: (his voice coming from far away) Always keep your eye on the ball, Cinderella!

COMPREHENSION QUESTIONS

Circle your answer.

1. What is a *cleat*?

    a. a dancing shoe

    b. a baseball shoe

    c. a lamp shade

    d. a kind of glove

2. What was unusual about Cinderella's cleats?

    a. They were the wrong size.

    b. They were too loose.

    c. They were made of black patent leather.

    d. They had ruffles on them.

3. What happened as Cinderella slid into home plate?

    a. Her uniform turned into a frilly dress.

    b. She was tagged out.

    c. She hurt her knee.

    d. She lost her baseball glove.

4. Who do you think Brendan might be?

    a. Cinderella's best friend

    b. Cinderella's cousin

    c. a parent of a team member

    d. the captain of the baseball team

5. Why did Cinderella have to walk home?

    a. Her bike was stolen.

    b. Her carriage turned into a pumpkin.

    c. Her bike turned into canned pumpkin.

    d. She gave her bike to Brendan.

Write a short answer.

6. Why didn't Cinderella's stepmother want her to play baseball?

    _____

    _____

7. What did Cinderella's outfit for the ball look like?

    _____

    _____

44

COMPREHENSION QUESTIONS

Think about the characters in the original Cinderella story. Then, compare and contrast them to the characters from the play.

CHARACTERS	COMPARE (SAME)	CONTRAST (DIFFERENT)
Stepmother from the story and Stepmother from the play	1. 2.	1. 2.
Stepsisters from the story and Mia and Janet	1. 2.	1. 2.
Prince Charming and Brendan	1. 2.	1. 2.
Cinderella from the story and Cinderella from the play	1. 2.	1. 2.

1. Who is your favorite character from the original Cinderella story? Why?

   _____

   _____

2. Who is your favorite character from the play? Why?

   _____

   _____

DIVIDE & CONQUER

Math

BACKGROUND

Long division can be intimidating. It's a complicated mix of multiplying, subtracting, and carrying down numbers. "Divide & Conquer" seeks to make the multistep concept of long division friendlier and more accessible by comparing the dividend to an old office building that must be demolished. The crew "launches" groups of threes at the building to keep whittling away the dividend, section by section.

WARM-UP ACTIVITY

Write a long division problem on the board. Show students how the division sign resembles one vertical side and one horizontal side of a building. Ask students if they were going to take this "building" down, using the divisor, how would they do it? Ask if they've ever seen a building being demolished. Buildings are brought down piece by piece . . . just like a long division problem! If you haven't used the phrase "Divide, multiply, subtract, and bring down" in math lessons, introduce it now. Next, distribute copies of the script. Ask students to read it on their own first.

Then, read it together. This play includes challenging vocabulary words, including some math terms, so be sure to introduce the vocabulary before a choral reading.

CASTING

The parts in the play are written for readers of different levels, from Level 1 Roles (struggling readers) to Level 4 Roles (advanced readers).

LEVEL 4 ROLES
Boss   Katie

LEVEL 3 ROLES
Mark   Caroline

LEVEL 2 ROLES
Anton   Manager

LEVEL 1 ROLES
Derek
Math Monitor (nonspeaking role)

DISCUSSION

- Do you think it is hard to divide big numbers? Why or why not?
- What does the phrase "divide and conquer" mean? Why is it a good motto for long division?
- Which school subject is difficult for you to tackle? Why?

VOCABULARY TO REVIEW

binoculars	divisor	dividend	conquer	panic
explosion	suggest	focused	release	remainder

CHARACTER EDUCATION CONNECTION

Discuss the process of solving a math problem and the patience required to succeed. In order to ensure a correct answer, you have to follow a procedure and check each step to make sure you haven't forgotten anything. Why would this be easy for some people and hard for others? Why do some people think math is easier than other subjects? Why do some people think it's harder?

SCIENCE CONNECTION

Discuss the scientific process of conducting an experiment. How is an experiment like a long division problem? (You do it step by step.) Compare the process of conducting an experiment to the process of solving a long division problem (divide, multiply, subtract, bring down).

COSTUME, PROP, AND SET DESIGN SUGGESTIONS

COSTUMES: Boss and Workers–jeans, plaid shirts, boots, work gloves, construction hats (available from party stores); Manager–suit; Math Monitor–all black or plain khaki pants with a white shirt

PROPS: Real or toy tool belts; binoculars for the Boss

SET DESIGN: Write-on/wipe-away board on an easel; let students create and decorate a cardboard building facade for the easel, cut a hole in the cardboard that is the same size as the board, and attach the facade to the board with duct tape; if desired, before the Manager says, "That's good work," the Math Monitor can point to the original number (17,892) and then knock down the "building" (board and easel)

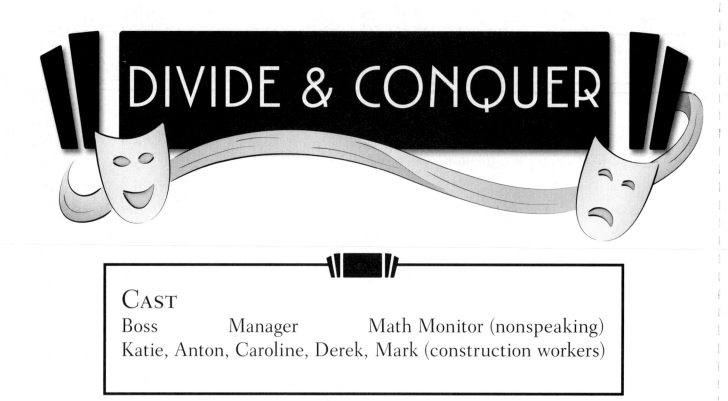

DIVIDE & CONQUER

> **CAST**
> Boss   Manager   Math Monitor (nonspeaking)
> Katie, Anton, Caroline, Derek, Mark (construction workers)

SETTING: *A building site on the Plain of Math. A crew is arriving to take down an old office building on the plain. They stand looking at the huge job in front of them. As the workers and boss discuss the problem, the Math Monitor keeps track of the problem on the board.*

KATIE: I've never seen an office building that big. This is impossible!

ANTON: I want to go home!

CAROLINE: Calm down, everyone. Wait until the boss gets here.

BOSS: Good morning, everyone! Wow, that's one big building. Could somebody please get me my binoculars?

DEREK: Here they are, Boss!

BOSS: Thanks. Let's see, it looks like we're dealing with . . . seventeen thousand, eight hundred ninety-two.

(MATH MONITOR: *Write 17,892.*)

MARK: What?! It's just too big, Boss. Can't they just build around it?

ANTON: (*hopefully*) Great idea . . . maybe they could build the mall with the office building right in the middle.

BOSS: No, it's our job to take it down. And, I have some news about that. Our divisor is going to be the number three.

(MATH MONITOR: *Draw the division symbol around the dividend and write the divisor, 3.*)

KATIE: Three! That's such a small number! Can we do it?

CAROLINE: Of course we can!

BOSS: What's our motto, everyone?

ALL: DIVIDE AND CONQUER!

BOSS: (*smiling*) That's right! OK, nobody panic. We can divide this dividend building with a three just as well as with any other number. We're just going to have to do it in sections like we always do. What's the rule?

ALL: Divide, multiply, subtract, and bring down!

BOSS: Good! Let's get to work! (*to Caroline*) Come over here.

CAROLINE: Me, Boss?

BOSS: Yes. Take a look at that first part of the building. How many threes do you think we should throw at it?

CAROLINE: (*thinking*) Well, we can't take down the one in the ten thousands place by itself because three won't go into one.

BOSS: Good thinking. So, what should we use on the seventeen?

CAROLINE: How about some fours?

DEREK: No, I think we need to use fives.

BOSS: I think you've forgotten something.

ANTON: Twos! As many as we can!

MARK: I agree! Let's just throw some twos at the building and get out of here.

BOSS: Any other ideas?

CAROLINE: We have to use threes because we're dividing by three. Let's use five of them. That will be fifteen.

(MATH MONITOR: Write 5 on the answer line above the 7.)

BOSS: That's right! Load them up and let them fly!

ANTON: *(covering eyes)* I can't look! Tell me what's going on.

DEREK: Wow! Look at that!

(MATH MONITOR: Write 15 under the 17.)

CAROLINE: The five threes took down almost the whole section.

(MATH MONITOR: Subtract 15 from 17.)

KATIE: But, there's still a two left standing!

BOSS: That's OK. We'll get it on the next round. So, if we bring that eight in the hundreds place down, what number are we going to divide and conquer next?

(MATH MONITOR: *Bring down the 8.*)

MARK: Twenty-eight. That's still HUGE.

ANTON: (*thinking*) Let's see . . . how about . . .

CAROLINE: How about attacking this section with nine threes? Nine times three is twenty-seven.

(MATH MONITOR: *Write 9 on the answer line above the 8.*)

BOSS: OK, team. Let's try it! Load up nine of those threes and release!

MARK: *(amazed)* Listen to that explosion!

ANTON: I think it's all going to come down!

(MATH MONITOR: *Write 27 under the 28.*)

DEREK: Not quite.

(MATH MONITOR: *Subtract 27 from 28.*)

BOSS: Hand me those binoculars, please. No, you are right. After the subtraction, there's still a one left standing. So, what do we do?

ALL: BRING IT DOWN!

(MATH MONITOR: *Bring down the 9.*)

BOSS: So, that means our next section is . . .

ANTON: Nineteen.

BOSS: Exactly. What do you suggest?

KATIE: Let's try to take two sections down at once. Attack the remaining one hundred ninety-two with one charge. Then, we could go eat lunch early.

DEREK: Would that be smart?

BOSS: I don't think so. Let's stay focused here. How many threes should we use for the nineteen section?

CAROLINE: How about six threes?

(MATH MONITOR: *Write 6 on the answer line above the 9.*)

BOSS: Because . . . ?

KATIE: That would be eighteen.

(**MATH MONITOR:** *Write 18 under the 19.*)

ANTON: *(yelling)* Let's give it a try!

DEREK: *(yelling)* Load those threes!

BOSS: *(calling out)* Let them fly!

(**MATH MONITOR:** *Subtract 18 from 19.*)

MARK: Wow. That worked . . . almost.

BOSS: There's only a one left standing. Well, team, what do you think?

CAROLINE: We're not going to let a one stand in our way.

BOSS: That's the spirit! What's the last number we have to bring down?

DEREK: A two.

(**MATH MONITOR:** *Bring down the 2.*)

BOSS: So, our last section to divide is a twelve. Any ideas?

KATIE: Wait a minute. Maybe we'll get to go to lunch early after all!

BOSS: Because . . . ?

CAROLINE: Because twelve can be divided by three evenly!

Boss: And that means . . . ?

All: NO REMAINDER!

Boss: That's right! We'll be all done after this. So, how many threes do we need to use this time?

Derek: Four!

Boss: (smiling) You will go far. Load those threes!

(**Math Monitor:** Write 4 on the answer line above the 2.)

Anton: Here they go! Cover your ears!

(**Math Monitor:** Write 12 under the 12.)

Katie: HOORAY!

(**Math Monitor:** Subtract 12 from 12.)

$$
\begin{array}{r}
5{,}964 \\
3\overline{)17{,}892} \\
-15 \\
\hline
28 \\
-27 \\
\hline
19 \\
-18 \\
\hline
12 \\
-12 \\
\hline
0
\end{array}
$$

MARK: The dividend building of seventeen thousand, eight hundred ninety-two is no more!

MANAGER: That's good work.

BOSS: Teamwork is a great thing.

MANAGER: So, are you ready for your next job?

KATIE: Um . . . after lunch, we will be.

MANAGER: It's a big job. We've got a dividend skyscraper to bring down. It's two hundred seventy-nine thousand, four hundred eighty-six. The head office is sending us two as a divisor.

BOSS: That's probably the biggest dividend we've ever worked on. What do you think, team?

CAROLINE: We can do it, Boss!

ALL: DIVIDE AND CONQUER!

COMPREHENSION QUESTIONS

Write a short answer.

1. What is the crew in "Divide and Conquer" trying to do?

   _____

   _____

   _____

2. What happens at the end of the play?

   _____

   _____

   _____

Circle your answer.

3. Look at the math problem at the end of the play. Will there be a remainder?

   YES   NO

4. Where does the play take place?

   a. Mathland

   b. Mathville

   c. The Plain of Math

   d. The Math Mountains

5. Which character is worried about eating lunch?

   a. Katie   c. Caroline

   b. Anton   d. Derek

6. Who is the leader of the team?

   a. Katie   c. The Manager

   b. The Boss   d. Mark

7. What does "Divide and Conquer" mean?

   a. Division is so hard that it has to be conquered.

   b. If you work at something one piece at a time, you can master it.

   c. Conquering math is easy if you use division.

8. What is a remainder?

   a. A number that is left over after the division problem is complete.

   b. A section of a building that cannot be knocked down.

   c. Leftover numbers that aren't used in the problem.

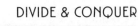
COMPREHENSION ACTIVITY

What do you think a dividend building looks like? Answer the questions below.

1. If the building had towers, would each number be a tower?   YES   NO

2. Would all of the towers be the same height?   YES   NO

3. Would the towers on your building have flags?   YES   NO

4. Write four other things that your building would have.

_____

_____

5. Now, draw your dividend building, using this number from the play: 279,486.

Try this: Pick one of the characters from "Divide and Conquer" and write a detailed description of that character. What does the character look like? What is he or she like? On a separate piece of paper, draw a picture of the character.

BLACKWATER MYSTERY

Science

BACKGROUND

This play is set in a swamp or wetland area. The campers are from an urban area, and they attend a day camp that allows them to explore a natural environment. The setting, which could be in any swamp or wetland area, offers the chance to study details about the environment and fossils. Use the information sheet on page 60 to introduce students to the interesting items the campers find in "Blackwater Mystery"—a sensitive plant, a cypress tree with knees, a piece of shale, and a trilobite.

WARM-UP ACTIVITY

Create a two- or three-clue mystery search in the classroom. Give students the first clue by writing it on the board or read it aloud to them. Then, have students suggest where you should look for the next clue. (With students as guides and you as the searcher, you will avoid the havoc of everyone searching at once.) Have the final clue end with some small surprise or treat for the class. Next, distribute copies of the

script and introduce the play. Ask students to read it on their own first. Then, read it together as a choral reading.

CASTING

The parts in the play are written for readers of different levels, from Level 1 Roles (struggling readers) to Level 4 Roles (advanced readers).

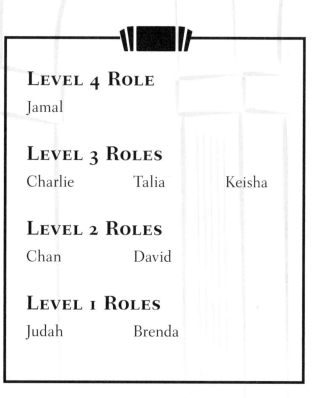

LEVEL 4 ROLE
Jamal

LEVEL 3 ROLES
Charlie   Talia   Keisha

LEVEL 2 ROLES
Chan   David

LEVEL 1 ROLES
Judah   Brenda

DISCUSSION

- Have you ever seen a swamp or wetland? What was it like?
- Have you ever been to camp? Tell the class about your experience at camp.
- Tell other students about a mystery story that you have read or heard. How did the characters solve the mystery?

VOCABULARY TO REVIEW

swamp	sensitive plant	oxygen	cypress	boulder
shale	sedimentary	fossil	trilobite	exoskeleton

WRITING CONNECTION

Have students write poems about a cypress tree. What is it like to live and thrive in a swamp? Have students write their poems from the tree's point of view.

SOCIAL STUDIES CONNECTION

How is life different for people who live in swamp or wetland areas? Encourage students to learn more about how people cope with wet ground (for example, by building houses on stilts), flooding, interesting wildlife, and other challenges of life in these areas. One story that is set in a swamp area is the classic book *The Yearling* by Marjorie Kinnan Rawlings (Simon Pulse, 1988). Share a segment of the book that describes the family's house or property as a springboard for discussion.

COSTUME, PROP, AND SET DESIGN SUGGESTIONS

COSTUMES: *Jamal* and *Campers*–camp T-shirts (use fabric paint to write "Blackwater Camp" on colorful T-shirts), shorts, sneakers

PROPS: Four small boxes; flashlight; stick; fossil or small rock to represent the trilobite

SET DESIGN: Artificial Christmas trees or ficus trees (borrowed from students and staff) can be placed around the stage, or large tree branches can be placed in large, disposable flowerpots and set in place with plaster; potted flowers set around the trees; flowerpots can be covered with lengths of brown fabric to represent dirt; rocks made from papier-mâché and painted gray; branches and artificial leaves strewn around to represent the forest floor; Meeting Hall: student-created sign that says "Blackwater Camp Meeting Hall," table in the center with a large, black papier-mâché rock

THE SENSITIVE PLANT is a member of the pea family. Its Latin name is *Mimosa pudica*. It is also commonly called a "Touch-Me-Not Plant." If you touch a sensitive plant, its leaves will close tightly and droop. If you touch it repeatedly, the stems will also droop. The plant will also do this at night if it gets cold. Left undisturbed for about 10 minutes, the leaves will open again and the stems will stand tall. Why does the plant do this? Probably as a defense against animals who might try to eat it. When the leaves droop, the plant's long thorns are exposed as a warning.

CYPRESS KNEES are stump-like protrusions in the swampy waters that surround cypress tree trunks. They are found in a variety of shapes, colors, and sizes. Some are up to 12' (approximately 3.75 m) tall. Cypress knees are extensions of the tree's root system that grow above the soil. The knees help brace the trees against winds and provide support in the unstable mud of the swampland. It is also believed that the knees act as "snorkels," helping to provide oxygen to the submerged roots.

SHALE is a type of sedimentary rock that is formed from tightly compacted clay. It is the most abundant type of sedimentary rock. Shale is found in many colors, but it is most often greenish-gray or grayish-black. Most shale resembles thin slices of rock pressed together and can be split into thin sheets.

A TRILOBITE is an extinct marine arthropod. Trilobite fossils can be found throughout the world. Trilobites lived in shallow seas and flourished for over 300 million years. The name "trilobite" means "three-lobed one" and refers to the three lobes of the head. The trilobite also had a three-segmented body. Interestingly, the trilobite was the earliest known animal to have the ability to see. Today, people collect trilobite fossils all over the world, and throughout history, the fossils were also collected and often worn as amulets or pendants.

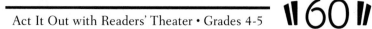

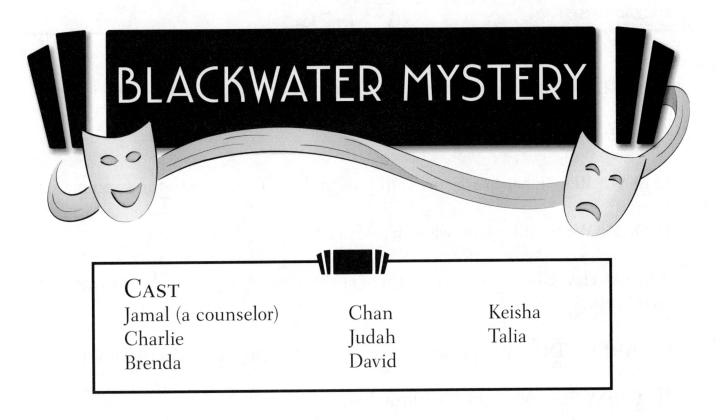

BLACKWATER MYSTERY

CAST

Jamal (a counselor)	Chan	Keisha
Charlie	Judah	Talia
Brenda	David	

SETTING: *A day camp. There is a big building with a crafts room, a meeting hall, and a kitchen. Outside, there are sports fields and nature trails. The nature trails border a marshland area that is home to many animals and birds.*

JAMAL: OK, everyone listen up! Tomorrow is our last day at camp. We'll be having a big picnic and games. But, this afternoon you have some free time to visit some of your favorite places at the camp.

CHAN: What can we do this afternoon?

JAMAL: You can play baseball or soccer. You can do crafts with Ms. Jenkins in the crafts room. Or, you can go on Nature Trail Number One. That's the one that is just outside of the sports fields. There was a big storm last night, so things are still a little wet. Be careful! Any questions?

KEISHA: No, Jamal. That sounds cool. See you later!

JAMAL: I'll be here helping Ms. Jenkins if anybody needs me.

CHARLIE: I want to go on the nature trail again. Who wants to go with me?

ALL: I do!

JAMAL: Remember to stay on Trail One and don't go off into the swamp areas.

JUDAH: We will! I mean, we won't!

TALIA: Hey, Charlie! Look over there at the edge of the path. What's that shiny metal thing?

CHARLIE: Did someone drop a can or something? We'd better pick it up.

BRENDA: It's not a can. It's a little box.

DAVID: Look at that. It almost looks like someone buried it.

JUDAH: Open it, Brenda!

BRENDA: There's a piece of paper inside.

DAVID: It's wrapped in plastic.

CHAN: What does it say?

KEISHA: (reading) "You found the first clue! Good job. Now, go to the place where our favorite plant grows . . . but touch it not!"

CHARLIE: A clue! Do you think Jamal left this for us?

BRENDA: What plant is it?

DAVID: (thinking) The clue says "touch it not."

TALIA: I know! It's the sensitive plant. Remember when Jamal showed it to us on our hike last week?

BRENDA: Yes! That must be it.

KEISHA: You're right! He said that it was also called a "touch-me-not." Let's go! It's down by the stream.

CHARLIE: There it is! It's that plant over there. Remember how the leaves curl up if you touch them?

BRENDA: So, be careful. Don't touch!

JUDAH: I will! I mean, I won't!

TALIA: If we aren't supposed to touch the plant, that must mean that the clue is hidden somewhere away from the plant.

CHAN: Good thinking, Talia. I'll look over here.

CHARLIE: I'll look along the path. David, why don't you look over there around that big tree.

DAVID: Look! I see something shiny!

BRENDA: Where?

KEISHA: I see it, too. Up in the notch of the tree. Good job, David.

CHARLIE: It's another little box. Wait, the lid is stuck.

CHAN: There's another paper inside.

CHARLIE: I'll read it. It says, "You are hot on the trail! Next, go to the place where there are no feet and no legs, but lots of knees. Good luck!"

JUDAH: What does that mean?

BRENDA: Think, everyone!

TALIA: How can there be knees with no legs?

DAVID: Maybe it doesn't mean real knees.

KEISHA: David, you're right! I bet that note is talking about cypress knees!

CHARLIE: What are those?

CHAN: That's right—Charlie, you were gone the day we saw those.

TALIA: Jamal took us to see this huge cypress tree. It's near the turnaround of the nature trail. And, it has its knees all around it.

 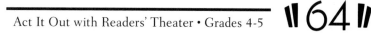

CHARLIE: Knees? How can a tree have knees?

JUDAH: The knees are roots.

BRENDA: That's right.

KEISHA: The roots grow these big bumps that come up from under the ground. Jamal said that because the knees are above the wet ground, they help the tree get oxygen to its roots.

JUDAH: Other trees don't have those.

TALIA: That's because cypress trees grow in swamps. The ground is half water, and it's hard for the tree to get rooted. The knees help the tree stay stable, too.

CHARLIE: OK, then! Take me to the knees!

DAVID: We're almost there.

BRENDA: There's the tree!

JUDAH: Watch out.

KEISHA: Judah's right. Remember, Jamal said that the ground is very soft around the tree. Don't leave the path!

CHARLIE: Where would Jamal have hidden that note? If we aren't supposed to leave the path, look along its edges.

CHAN: *(calling out)* What's this over here?

DAVID: I don't see anything.

KEISHA: Oh, there's a tiny little silver spot. The rain washed the dirt away from it. Otherwise, we would never have seen it.

CHAN: It's buried really deep.

JUDAH: Dig!

CHARLIE: This one is even harder to open than the other ones. Talia, see if you can do it.

TALIA: Here's the note! It's wrapped up like the other ones. It says, "For your big surprise, find the black rock at Blackwater."

CHAN: (thinking) The black rock . . .

BRENDA: There's a big rock beside the baseball field.

KEISHA: Yes, but that's a granite boulder. It's not black, it's pink and gray.

DAVID: There are lots of rocks on the path.

CHARLIE: But, this sounds like an important rock . . . one we should know about. One that we've talked about . . .

JUDAH: I know! The one in the meeting hall!

TALIA: Good job, Judah! It's that big piece of shale in the meeting hall. It's there to show us what a sedimentary rock looks like.

CHAN: It has cracks in it.

CHARLIE: Yes, between the layers of rock. Those would be great hiding places. Come on, everyone . . . let's go!

BRENDA: The hall is empty.

KEISHA: Judah, grab that flashlight. Let's take a closer look.

DAVID: I see something shiny!

CHARLIE: Here, Keisha. Here's a stick. See if you can pry the box out. It's really stuck down in there.

KEISHA: I've got it!

CHARLIE: OK! Let's see what surprise Jamal has hidden for us.

JUDAH: What does the note say?

CHARLIE: (*reading*) "Dear Jamal, You've been a great friend to me. I'm really going to miss you. Here is something that you've always wanted. I hope it brings you good luck. Your friend, Lee"

BRENDA: Lee? Who's Lee?

TALIA: And the note is written to Jamal, not to us! What's going on here?

CHAN: What else is in the box?

CHARLIE: It looks like a beetle. Only it's carved out of stone.

JAMAL: Hi, everyone! What have you been doing this afternoon?

JUDAH: We found this.

JAMAL: (*smiling*) Wow! That's a trilobite. You found that on the nature path?

BRENDA: No, we found it in this little metal box.

TALIA: What's a trilobite?

JAMAL: This is an ancient sea animal. It lived in shallow salt water, millions of years ago. Now, it's a fossil. See all of those ridges? That's called an exoskeleton. It had a skeleton on the outside of its body.

JUDAH: Did it live around here?

JAMAL: No. A lot of trilobites have been found in Idaho. There was a big, shallow sea there. This is what's called a replacement fossil. Minerals have replaced the living thing. So, it looks like it's been turned into stone. I used to know someone who had one of these.

CHARLIE: Was his name Lee?

JAMAL: (*surprised*) How in the world did you know that?

DAVID: He left this for you. Look at the note.

CHAN: We found it in the shale.

BRENDA: We found lots of clues.

CHARLIE: And the clues led us here. What happened to Lee? And how come you didn't find the clues yourself?

JAMAL: (*shaking his head*) You know, he hinted that he had a big surprise for me, but I never found out what it was. I met Lee when we were campers here. Then, his dad found a job in another city. We were going to spend our last day of camp together. But, his family ended up leaving early, and Lee didn't get to come back to camp. These clues have been hidden here for a long time!

BRENDA: How long?

JAMAL: *(softly)* Ten years.

TALIA: I bet that big storm last night washed away some of the topsoil. That's how we found the first box! It must have been buried before.

KEISHA: Well, now you have your very own trilobite, Jamal.

CHARLIE: And you know what surprise Lee planned for you.

JAMAL: He was a good friend. I miss him. Thanks, everyone!

CHAN: There's the bus. It's time to go home.

JAMAL: OK. Remember, tomorrow is the big picnic. We're going to have a cookout, races, a baseball game, and our last big camp meeting of the year. So, have a safe trip home and don't forget about the picnic tomorrow!

JUDAH: We will! I mean, we won't!

COMPREHENSION QUESTIONS

Circle your answer.

1. What is a *trilobite*?

    a. a beetle

    b. an ancient sea creature

    c. a type of rock

    d. a plant with leaves that curl up

2. Which of these is a sedimentary rock?

    a. granite   c. shale

    b. marble   d. basalt

3. Why did the clues survive so long?

    a. They were wrapped in plastic and put in metal boxes.

    b. They were hidden in safe places, like piggy banks and desk drawers.

    c. They were buried in plastic boxes.

    d. They were written on special paper.

4. What is a cypress knee?

    a. a kind of branch

    b. an underground root

    c. a big knothole

    d. an above-ground bump on a root

5. What do cypress knees do for the tree?

    a. They make the tree bend over.

    b. They help the roots breathe and keep the tree stable.

    c. They help the roots tunnel underground.

    d. They help the tree float on the water.

Write a short answer.

6. Why didn't Jamal find the clues a long time ago?

    _____

    _____

    _____

    _____

7. What was Lee like? How do you know?

    _____

    _____

    _____

    _____

COMPREHENSION QUESTIONS

Put the following events from the story in order. Write numbers 1-7 in the blanks.

_____ The campers find a box in the layers of shale.

_____ The campers run to the meeting hall.

_____ Talia sees a shiny piece of metal near the nature trail path.

_____ The campers show Jamal the trilobite.

_____ Jamal reads Lee's note.

_____ The campers head to the sensitive plant.

_____ David finds a clue in the notch of a tree.

What do you think Camp Blackwater looks like? Draw a map on a separate piece of paper. Use the directions below to help you.

1. Draw the camp buildings. Make sure to include the big building with the crafts room, kitchen, and meeting hall.

2. Draw the surrounding areas of marshlands, woods, and nature trails.

3. Draw and label the following: meeting hall, sensitive plant, cypress tree, Nature Trail Number One, baseball field.

4. Number the place where the campers found the first clue with a 1. Number their next stop with a 2 and keep numbering until you get to the place where they talked to Jamal at the end. Use the answers from above to help you.

5. Now, draw a dotted line to connect the campers' stops to show their complete path.

FIRST & LAST DAYS

Social Studies

BACKGROUND

"First and Last Days" is based on two actual historical events and how they impacted a Virginia family named McLean. It is an amazing fact of history that the first battle of the Civil War and the war's final surrender both took place on the property of Wilmer McLean, Sr., a businessman and farmer. After the battle of Bull Run, which started on the McLean property, Mr. McLean moved his family to safety in central Virginia . . . only to find the war on his doorstep again in 1865. The characters in the play are based on real people.

WARM-UP ACTIVITY

If you haven't discussed the Civil War with students, give a brief overview of the facts: how the war started, why it was fought, and how it concluded. (Use the information sheet on page 74.) You can also use the Internet and library resources to find pictures and paintings that show the people in carriages who drove out to "watch the war" on the McLean property. Visit the Web site for the Appomattox Court House McLean home. The site shows photos of the house and parlor, along with items that are on display there. (The house is now a museum.) Next, distribute copies of the script and introduce the play. Ask students to read it on their own first. Then, read it together as a choral reading.

CASTING

The parts in the play are written for readers of different levels, from Level 1 Roles (struggling readers) to Level 4 Roles (advanced readers).

LEVEL 4 ROLES

Narrator   Mr. McLean

LEVEL 3 ROLES

Maria   Mrs. McLean   Wilmer, Jr.

LEVEL 2 ROLES

Ocie   Colonel Marshall   General Lee

LEVEL 1 ROLES

Lulu

General Grant (nonspeaking role)

DISCUSSION

- What made the Civil War different from other wars in which the United States has fought?
- What do you think it would be like to have a battle begin near your home? What do you think your family would do if that happened?
- Discuss how people must have felt at the end of the Civil War. Why would there be different feelings about the end of the war in different parts of the country?

VOCABULARY TO REVIEW

parlor	flee	property	shell (exploding)	handsome
Confederate	raid	retreat	surrender	aide
colonel	general	weapons		

SCIENCE CONNECTION

Talk about the impact of a battle on the plants and animals in the area. What would happen to crops in a field and to the animals' homes in the woods? What would the area look like after a battle?

WRITING CONNECTION

Write about the surrender in the McLean's parlor from the viewpoint of Lulu's rag doll, which was left on the sofa. What did she "see" and "hear?"

COSTUME, PROP, AND SET DESIGN SUGGESTIONS

COSTUMES: *Mr. McLean*–dark pants, light dress shirt, suspenders, bow tie, jacket, glasses, powder to make hair gray or white, dark boots; *Mrs. McLean*–blouse with collar, floor-length skirt, dark boots, powder to make hair gray or white, hair in bun, glasses; *Maria* and *Lulu*–long dresses, dark tights, dark boots; *Wilmer, Jr.* and *Ocie*–dress shirts, dark pants, dark boots, suspenders, golf caps; *Narrator*–suit or dress; *General Grant*–blue jacket, black pants, blue hat, brown hair (or wig), brown beard; *General Lee*–gray jacket, black pants, red sash around waist, gray hat, powder to whiten hair, white beard; *Colonel Marshall*–tattered gray jacket, black pants

PROPS: Overnight bags for family members; rag doll for Lulu

SET DESIGN: Loveseat alone on stage for first part of play; when the Narrator takes the action back in time, add end tables, hurricane lamps, coffee table, afghan over back of loveseat, doll on loveseat, and rug on floor (Soldiers should take these additional items as they exit the stage at the end, leaving only the loveseat.)

THE CIVIL WAR (1861–1865) was the bloodiest war in America's history. More than 3 million Americans fought in the war, and over 600,000—two percent of the nation's population—died.

WHAT CAUSED THE CIVIL WAR?

The most common answer to this question is slavery. Slavery was the only institution found in the South but not in the North. There was also disagreement about extending slavery into new western states. In addition to slavery, the North and South disagreed about states' rights. The South believed that states should have more individual control, but the North believed the federal government should have more power. Finally, the states disagreed about tariffs (taxes on goods brought in from other countries). Because the North had a lot of factories, they didn't want outside goods brought in; they wanted to sell their own goods without any competition. The South, however, wanted to send their crops overseas to sell and buy foreign goods cheaply.

HOW DID THE WAR BEGIN?

Confederate troops in South Carolina demanded the surrender of Fort Sumter. The Union Army refused and shots were fired. Two days later, the fort was surrendered. The next and first major battle of the war was the First Battle of Bull Run. (Southerners called it the First Battle of Manassas.) This was a bizarre battle. Hundreds of people followed the Union soldiers to the battle site. They set up picnics and sat down to watch the action. This battle took place on the farm of Wilmer McLean, Sr. When the bullets began to fly, it was chaos as people began to run. McLean and his family had vacated their house only one day earlier, knowing that the area would be unsafe.

WHO WERE THE LEADERS OF THE ARMIES?

General Ulysses S. Grant was the commander of the Union army. He was an unassuming man, known for his extreme determination and calmness. After the war, he served two terms as President of the United States.

General Robert E. Lee was the commander of the Confederate army. Interestingly, President Lincoln first offered him the command of the Union army, but he refused. Lee was a very capable field commander who was known for his remarkable strategic ability.

HOW DID THE WAR END?

After four long years of war, the two armies were exhausted and battered. Following a 10-month siege of Richmond, Virginia, the capital of the Confederacy, supplies were running low and General Lee ordered his troops to retreat. General Grant realized the opportunity to force a surrender and chased the retreating army. For six days, the army retreated until reaching Appomattox Court House. General Grant offered to accept General Lee's surrender and a meeting place was established. The two generals met in the parlor of Wilmer McLean's home and discussed the conditions of the surrender for one and a half hours. For all practical purposes, the war ended that day, April 9, 1865.

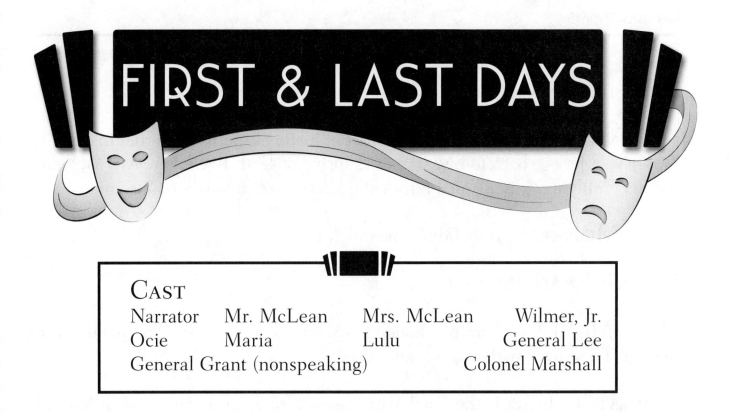

FIRST & LAST DAYS

Cast

Narrator	Mr. McLean	Mrs. McLean	Wilmer, Jr.
Ocie	Maria	Lulu	General Lee
General Grant (nonspeaking)		Colonel Marshall	

SETTING: *1865. A large, comfortable parlor in a 19th century home. There is a patterned carpet on the floor, a black, horsehair sofa in one corner, and paintings on the walls. There is a large fireplace. The room is oddly empty and messy.*

MARIA: Well, at least they didn't take the sofa. I suppose it was too heavy!

LULU: Where's my doll? I left her on the sofa! Now, she's gone.

MRS. MCLEAN: Lulu, I am so sorry to tell you this, but a soldier took your doll. He called it "the silent witness." I'll make you another doll. I promise.

MR. MCLEAN: They took everything that wasn't nailed down! I would never have offered our house to them if I'd known this would happen.

WILMER, JR.: But think about what happened here, Papa. It's amazing.

MR. MCLEAN: I think I'd rather be less amazed and still have all of our furniture . . . and Lulu's doll.

LULU: *(crying)* I want my doll!

OCIE: Don't cry, little sister. Your doll is a part of history now.

NARRATOR: The McLean family is part of history now, too. In order to explain it all to you, let's go back four years to the spring of 1861. Back then, Mr. McLean and his family were living on a farm called Yorkshire in northern Virginia.

MRS. MCLEAN: Husband! Come quickly!

MR. MCLEAN: What is it, my dear?

MRS. MCLEAN: Our neighbors have sent a messenger. The armies are coming! They are less than a day away.

NARRATOR: In 1861, the Civil War was just about to begin. And, it started right in Mr. McLean's front yard.

MR. MCLEAN: Wilmer, help your sisters carry things out to the carriage. We have to leave right now!

WILMER, JR.: But Papa, I want to watch the battle. There are people driving into the fields—city people. They are planning to watch. Why can't we?

OCIE: You should see them, Papa. They have picnic baskets and everything!

MR. MCLEAN: Well, those people are fools. Haven't they ever seen a gun fired before? These soldiers aren't coming here to watch birds or have a picnic. They are coming to fight!

MRS. MCLEAN: We must leave quickly, children. We will go to Cousin William's place until the fighting is over.

MARIA: And can we come home when the war is over?

MR. MCLEAN: Let's hope that this one battle will decide the matter.

NARRATOR: But that first battle, called Bull Run by the Northerners and First Manassas by the Southerners, was only the beginning of the fighting. The people who had lined up their carriages to watch the fighting ended up fleeing for their lives. The McLean family left one day before the battle started. When Mr. and Mrs. McLean came back, they found their farm in ruins.

MRS. MCLEAN: Thank goodness we didn't bring the children. The soldiers are still burying the dead.

MR. MCLEAN: Jennie, there isn't a fence left on the farm. They were all torn down in the battle. The crops are ruined, and the summer kitchen is gone.

MRS. MCLEAN: (*shocked*) Gone?! How did that happen?

MR. MCLEAN: It looks like an exploding shell went right through it. It seems that the fighting started right here—right in front of the porch. The first shot of the battle went right past our parlor window.

MRS. MCLEAN: Wil, we cannot bring the children back here. What are we going to do?

MR. MCLEAN: I believe all of the fighting will be here, near Washington, D.C. I'll ride south and look at some property further away from the fighting. We will have to move to get away from the war.

NARRATOR: Mr. McLean found a new farm in central Virginia near a quiet little town. It was a peaceful place. He brought his family to see it.

LULU: What a big house!

MARIA: I think it's a very handsome house with all of that red brick. Do you think so, too, Mother?

MRS. MCLEAN: Yes, I do, though we will have to do some painting and cleaning. But best of all, it's a nice, quiet little town. The war will surely never come here.

NARRATOR: Mrs. McLean was wrong about that, though she wouldn't know it for several years. Let's visit the McLean family in the early spring of 1865.

WILMER, JR.: *(calling out)* Mother! The battle is coming closer! Listen to the guns and horses!

MRS. MCLEAN: Can this be true?

MR. MCLEAN: Yes, Jennie, it is. Our army is in retreat. General Lee may be about to surrender. But, the fighting still goes on . . . and it's just west of our little town of Appomattox Court House.

MARIA: Papa! The fighting is coming to our house? Again?

OCIE: Let's hope that if there is going to be another battle, it doesn't start in our front yard again!

NARRATOR: Mr. McLean went to the main street of the small town to see if he could hear some news. As he walked down the road, two soldiers on horseback passed him. One of them, Colonel Marshall, was General Lee's aide.

COLONEL MARSHALL: Sir, perhaps you could help us.

MR. MCLEAN: What is it, Colonel?

COLONEL MARSHALL: I must ask you to keep this a secret. But, General Lee has asked to meet with General Grant to talk about . . . well, to discuss some matters. And I have been sent into this town to find a house where these two gentlemen can meet and talk.

MR. MCLEAN: There is an empty house just ahead here. The family who lived here left about a year ago.

NARRATOR: The Colonel got down from his horse and looked in the windows of the empty house.

COLONEL MARSHALL: There is no furniture here. I cannot bring the two leaders of this war to meet in an empty room.

MR. MCLEAN: No, I guess not. Well, sir, I can offer you the parlor of my own home, if that might suit you better.

NARRATOR: Colonel Marshall went with Mr. McLean to the big, comfortable brick home. And he agreed that the parlor, with its fine furniture and paintings, was a much better meeting place.

LULU: General Lee is coming here?

MARIA: And General Grant?

MRS. McLEAN: Yes, girls. Your father has offered our home as a meeting place for the two generals. We will have to wait outside while they talk.

OCIE: Mama! Look outside! There are soldiers coming up the road!

NARRATOR: It was April 9, 1865—Palm Sunday, the Sunday before Easter. And, as the McLean family watched, part of the Confederate army was streaming across their land and coming into their front yard.

WILMER, JR.: *(hushed voice)* Look! It's General Lee.

GENERAL LEE: Are you Mr. McLean?

MR. McLEAN: Yes, General, I am.

GENERAL LEE: Thank you for allowing us to use your home. Good afternoon, Mrs. McLean.

MRS. MCLEAN: Good afternoon, General.

LULU: Mama, I left my doll inside!

MRS. MCLEAN: Hush, Lulu. You can get it later.

NARRATOR: About half an hour later, the McLean family heard horses coming down the road toward the house. And there was General Grant with his officers. The Confederate soldiers looked at him silently. He nodded to the McLean family and went inside.

MR. MCLEAN: (quietly) So, here we are, sitting on our porch, waiting to see if the war has really ended.

LULU: How can it end here?

WILMER, JR.: The generals will talk. If they agree to stop fighting, then the war will officially be over.

MR. MCLEAN: Look at that! Those soldiers are pulling the cannons right across our fields. The corn will be ruined.

MARIA: (nervously) Why are they bringing the cannons here?

MRS. MCLEAN: Because if General Lee surrenders, he will have to give General Grant all of his weapons . . . and that includes the cannons.

OCIE: I wonder how long it will take?

NARRATOR: It took less than an hour. The war that had dragged on for so many years ended with a simple agreement and a handshake. General Lee walked out of the house and spoke briefly to his soldiers.

GENERAL LEE: Men, we have fought through this long war together. I have done the best that I could for you.

NARRATOR: After the generals had gone, other soldiers started to raid the parlor, taking furniture and other things to remember the historic event. They even took Lulu's rag doll.

MRS. MCLEAN: What a mess! I can't believe that those soldiers acted like this. Where are their manners?

MARIA: Their heads must be spinning, Mama. Think of it. The war is over! They can all finally go home now. They're not thinking about anything else.

MR. MCLEAN: Wilmer, why are you smiling? Our house and our fields are destroyed—again!

WILMER, JR.: I just realized something, Papa. The war started in our front yard, and it ended in our parlor!

COMPREHENSION QUESTIONS

Circle your answer.

1. What is the youngest McLean child's name?

   a. Ocie

   b. Maria

   c. Wilmer, Jr.

   d. Lulu

2. Where did the McLean family live in 1861?

   a. a town called Appomattox Court House

   b. a farm called Yorkshire

   c. a village called Bull Run

   d. a plantation called Tara

3. Why did the McLean family move?

   a. They wanted a nicer house.

   b. They wanted a safer place to live.

   c. They wanted a better view of the battles.

   d. They wanted a bigger farm.

Write a short answer.

4. Why did the soldiers take things from the McLean home?

   _____

   _____

   _____

5. Who were the two generals who came to the home to talk?

   _____

   _____

   _____

Circle your answer.

6. What is a *parlor*?

   a. a bedroom

   b. a living room

   c. a type of kitchen

7. What is a *surrender*?

   a. a competition

   b. an agreement to start fighting

   c. an agreement to stop fighting

COMPREHENSION QUESTIONS

Imagine that you are Maria or Wilmer McLean, Jr. You have been keeping a journal about the events of the Civil War. Read the description for each date below. Then, write a brief journal entry to describe each event.

1. July 4, 1861 (Two weeks before the battle of Bull Run, also known as First Manassas)

   _____

   _____

   _____

2. July 15, 1861 (The day your family leaves to escape the fighting that will begin tomorrow)

   _____

   _____

   _____

3. July 23, 1861 (A few days after the battle ends, when your father announces you're moving)

   _____

   _____

   _____

4. April 9, 1865 (The day of the surrender, when the generals meet in your parlor)

   _____

   _____

   _____

5. April 10, 1865 (The day after the surrender as you survey the damage to your home)

   _____

   _____

   _____

A PERFECT LIFE

Social Studies

BACKGROUND

"A Perfect Life" is a play about a real artist who overcame a disability. George Inness (1825–1894) had epilepsy. It was unusual in the 19th century for an epileptic to live to the age of 69. During his life, Inness painted and traveled extensively. At the time, doctors thought that epileptics should be kept quietly at home to avoid having seizures, but Inness fearlessly traveled across the United States and Europe to find subjects for his landscape paintings. He died in Scotland while watching a sunset. Inness's paintings can be found in museums throughout the United States and in the White House.

WARM-UP ACTIVITY

Use the Internet or library resources to find a picture of Inness's "The Lackawanna Valley." Show the painting to students. Explain that it was painted when railroads were still being built across the country. Point out the figure of the boy on the hillside. What might he be thinking? How will the trains change the countryside that he knows? Introduce the vocabulary words and briefly discuss epilepsy. Next, distribute copies of the script and introduce the play. Ask students to read it on their own first. Then, read it together as a choral reading.

CASTING

The parts in the play are written for readers of different levels, from Level 1 Roles (struggling readers) to Level 4 Roles (advanced readers).

LEVEL 4 ROLES
Narrator #2   Mr. Inness

LEVEL 3 ROLES
George   Narrator #1
Regis Gignoux   Museum Guide

LEVEL 2 ROLES
Mrs. Inness   Elizabeth
Railroad President

LEVEL 1 ROLES
Junk Shop Owner   Student

DISCUSSION

- What does it mean to have a disability? What are some examples of disabilities?
- How would George Inness's life have been different if he had listened to his parents and followed their advice?
- What are some of the advantages of working as an artist? What are some of the difficulties of this kind of life?

VOCABULARY TO REVIEW

epilepsy	seizure	frail	portrait
landscape	reasonable	gallery	roundhouse

SOCIAL STUDIES CONNECTION

Discuss the impact of the railroad system in the United States. How long did it take to build trains across the country? What did it mean to a town that was in a remote area to suddenly have a train nearby? How would things change? Research some examples and share them with the class.

MATH CONNECTION

Compare the speed of a horse and wagon (about 4 miles per hour) to a train. (Early trains traveled at a speed of about 25 miles per hour.) Choose two towns in a region of the United States and determine the distance between them by using a map. How long would it take to travel from one town to the other by horse and wagon? How long would it take by train in the 19th century?

COSTUME, PROP, AND SET DESIGN SUGGESTIONS

COSTUMES: *Narrators*–dresses or suits; *Others*–Since this play spans several decades (1820-1890), have students research clothing for each decade and brainstorm ways to duplicate the clothing for the play; *Museum Guide*–tan pants, white dress shirt, blue blazer; *Student*–age-appropriate clothes

PROPS: Envelope; painted pieces of foam display board to represent paintings; paintbrushes and pieces of partially painted foam board for George to carry with him when he travels to paint

SET DESIGN: Grocery Store–tables for shelves; baskets for displaying "products;" large, student-made signs to display when George travels–"New York City," "France," "Lackawanna Valley," "California," "Mexico," and "Washington, D.C." (scenes take place in these places; if you wish, display signs for all locations in the play to demonstrate George's extensive travels); Junk Shop–serapes on the walls; sombreros and maracas on tables; frames cut from foam board painted gold and silver; "painting" from previous scene; Museum Scene–foam board "paintings" suspended from fishing line

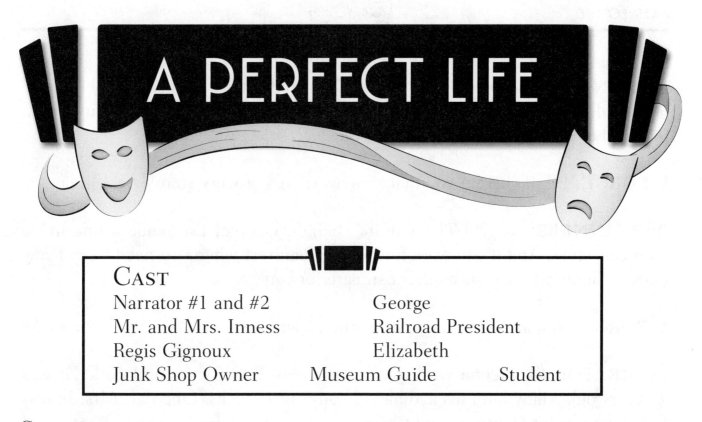

A PERFECT LIFE

Cast

Narrator #1 and #2   George
Mr. and Mrs. Inness   Railroad President
Regis Gignoux   Elizabeth
Junk Shop Owner   Museum Guide   Student

SETTING: *A grocery store in Newark, New Jersey, which was a farming town in the early 19th century. The store is owned by Mr. Inness. One of his sons, George, is in the store with him.*

NARRATOR #1: The Inness family lived well in the 1830s. Mr. Inness owned a grocery store, a farm, and some other businesses. Mr. and Mrs. Inness were the proud parents of 13 children. But, one of their sons, George, worried them.

NARRATOR #2: George had epilepsy, a disease that often made him weak and tired. Sometimes, George had seizures that scared his parents. In the 1800s, people were scared of epilepsy. There were no drugs or treatments to help people who had it.

MR. INNESS: George, I want you to help me in the store. There will be no more talk of you becoming a painter.

GEORGE: But, Father, I don't want to work in the store! I want to study art. Please let me go to New York City.

MR. INNESS: George, I can't do that. You couldn't even finish school because of your illness. You can't travel, not even to New York City. Why, if you worked too hard or traveled too far, you could die!

GEORGE: I'll die here if you make me work in a grocery store!

MR. INNESS: *(angry)* That's quite enough, George! I've made a fine living with this store. And if you work for me, you can rest when you need to and stay close to home where your mother can care for you.

GEORGE: *(quietly but firmly)* No, Father, I will not.

NARRATOR #1: George wrote to places in New York City to find work. He was 16 years old. Many boys his age had already started jobs. One day, Mrs. Inness found a letter for George in the mail.

MRS. INNESS: *(calling out)* George! A letter has come for you.

GEORGE: It's from Sherman and Smith! It's a mapmaking company. They are going to give me a job!

MRS. INNESS: A job? George, you already have a very good job. You are working in the grocery store.

GEORGE: But, Mother, if I work for Sherman and Smith, I can draw and paint maps all day. And in the evenings, I can go to art classes.

NARRATOR #2: George's mother told him that he was too frail to live in the big city. But, George went there anyway and worked very hard. Soon, he became too ill to keep working and studying. He came back home.

MRS. INNESS: You see, George? I was right!

MR. INNESS: You need to listen to us, George. We know what is best for you. You can always paint and draw quietly at home.

GEORGE: I'm sorry, Father, but I just don't want to do that.

MR. INNESS: *(just thinking of this)* Say! Maybe you can paint the portraits of some of our neighbors. That would make for a nice change, wouldn't it? They could come right here to our home.

GEORGE: I don't want to paint portraits. I want to paint landscapes.

MRS. INNESS: Landscapes?!

GEORGE: I want to travel to Europe and maybe even to California! I want to paint Niagara Falls. I want to paint in Italy.

MR. INNESS: George, be reasonable. You can't even travel to New York City and stay in good health. Why, landscape painters have to stand for hours when they paint outside. They have to travel for hundreds of miles to paint mountains or the ocean. You can't do that.

GEORGE: Yes, I can!

NARRATOR #1: George painted and drew by himself for three years. Then, he set out for New York City again. This time, he studied with a painter named Regis Gignoux.

GEORGE: *(calling out)* Mr. Gignoux! One of my paintings is going to be shown at the National Academy!

REGIS GIGNOUX: George, that is splendid! What an honor. And you are only 20 years old.

GEORGE: I am 20, but I haven't been to Europe yet! I need to study in Italy. I need to see the paintings in Paris.

REGIS GIGNOUX: Yes, all of that would be wonderful, George, but you are already very talented. I think you will do great things with your painting.

GEORGE: Thank you, Mr. Gignoux. I know I haven't been able to study with you for very long, but I've learned a lot.

NARRATOR #2: Even though his parents were horrified, George did travel to Europe. He used the money he had made from selling a painting. He loved studying the paintings he saw in France. When he returned to America, he met a young woman named Elizabeth Hart. They married in 1850.

GEORGE: Elizabeth, you know that artists don't make much money. And I am not in good health.

ELIZABETH: That doesn't matter to me, George. I believe in you. I think you will be a great painter.

NARRATOR #1: George had another person who believed in him, a man named Ogden Haggerty. Mr. Haggerty sent George and Elizabeth to Italy. George painted landscapes for Mr. Haggerty. George and Elizabeth lived in Italy for one and a half years. When they returned to America, George had to find new ways to make money.

GEORGE: (calling out) Elizabeth! Great news!

ELIZABETH: What is it, George?

GEORGE: The president of the new Lackawanna Railroad wants me to do a painting for him. They just built a roundhouse in the valley. He wants me to go there and paint it.

ELIZABETH: That is way out in the country, George. Are you sure you can do it? It won't be like traveling in Europe where there are good roads and trains.

GEORGE: Of course I can do it!

NARRATOR #2: George painted his picture of the Lackawanna Valley and the new roundhouse. He went to show it to the president of the railroad.

RAILROAD PRESIDENT: What is this?

GEORGE: It's your painting, sir.

RAILROAD PRESIDENT: But, this isn't what I wanted! I want a painting that shows our beautiful trains and our brand new roundhouse.

GEORGE: There's the roundhouse right there.

RAILROAD PRESIDENT: But . . . it's tiny. And where are all of my trains?

GEORGE: There's one of your trains right there. And there's another one way in the distance near the roundhouse.

‖92‖

RAILROAD PRESIDENT: You can hardly see the trains! And what are all of these tree stumps? There's a whole hill of them.

GEORGE: But that's what I saw when I went there. You see, this isn't just a painting of your railroad. It's a painting that shows how your railroad is going to change things.

RAILROAD PRESIDENT: What do you mean?

GEORGE: You built a railroad roundhouse far away in the countryside of Pennsylvania. Now, people are cutting down trees and getting ready to build a town. And that's what is going to happen wherever your railroad goes.

RAILROAD PRESIDENT: But . . . instead of showing off my shiny trains and my new roundhouse, you painted a bunch of ugly tree stumps!

GEORGE: (sighing) I painted you a picture of the future, sir. That's what trains are . . . the future of the United States.

NARRATOR #1: The railroad president was not the only one who didn't understand George's paintings. Throughout his life, George never made much money. There were long periods of time when he was ill and could not paint. But, he kept going. He did everything that his parents told him he would never be able to do.

NARRATOR #2: Other painters admired his talent. In the 1860s, he was elected to the National Academy. That was one of the highest honors that a painter could achieve in those days.

GEORGE: Elizabeth, I am ready to travel some more. I think we should go back to Italy for a while.

NARRATOR #1: George and Elizabeth lived in Italy again for four years. He sent his paintings to a gallery in Boston where they were sold.

NARRATOR #2: And later, George traveled some more in America, too. He painted Niagara Falls. He toured Florida. And finally, he was able to go out west to California where he painted the mountains of Yosemite.

ELIZABETH: George, you look tired. Shouldn't we stay home and rest?

GEORGE: I can't ask the landscapes to come to me! You know, my father thought I should paint portraits. That way, I could sit in the house all day long. But that's not what I wanted to do.

NARRATOR #1: George and Elizabeth went on a trip to Mexico. And there, they had a big surprise.

ELIZABETH: Look at this funny little junk shop, George. Let's go inside.

JUNK SHOP OWNER: May I help you?

GEORGE: Is that a painting stuck behind those old frames? What is that?

JUNK SHOP OWNER: It is a painting. A very nice painting. I will sell it to you for a few dollars. How about five dollars?

ELIZABETH: Why, George! It's your painting of the Lackawanna Valley!

GEORGE: *(laughing)* I guess that railroad president really didn't like this painting at all!

ELIZABETH: At least now we can buy it back!

NARRATOR #2: George never became a rich man during his lifetime, but now his paintings are worth thousands of dollars. And, you can see his work in famous museums around the world.

NARRATOR #1: Let's take a look in the National Gallery in Washington, D.C. Here is a tour guide with a school group.

MUSEUM GUIDE: And here is one of our most important American paintings. It is "The Lackawanna Valley" by George Inness.

STUDENT: What's that building way off in the valley?

MUSEUM GUIDE: That is the roundhouse of the Lackawanna Railroad. And see how the farmers have started to clear land and build? This painting shows us how the railroads changed the nation's landscape forever.

STUDENT: Who was George Inness?

MUSEUM GUIDE: He was a very brave man. Even though he had epilepsy, he traveled and painted and lived the life he wanted to live. And we're lucky that he did. If he didn't, we would not have wonderful paintings like this one to show us what the country was like in the 1800s.

COMPREHENSION QUESTIONS

Match the words to their meanings. Write the letters in the blanks.

_____ 1. Ogden Haggerty

_____ 2. Regis Gignoux

_____ 3. Elizabeth Hart

_____ 4. portrait

_____ 5. epilepsy

_____ 6. landscape

a. a disease that causes seizures

b. man who sent George to Italy

c. a painting of a person

d. wife of George Inness

e. art teacher

f. a painting of the countryside

Write a short answer.

7. Why do you think the author titled this play "A Perfect Life?"

_____

_____

8. How did George Inness's parents feel about him becoming a painter?

_____

_____

9. List four places to which George Inness traveled so that he could paint.

_____

_____

10. Based on the clues in the play, write a short description of the painting, *The Lackawanna Valley.*

_____

_____

COMPREHENSION ACTIVITY

Imagine you have decided to become an artist. Answer the questions below to help you plan your career.

1. Circle the type of artist that you hope to become.

   a. landscape painter

   b. portrait painter

   c. video artist

   d. cartoonist

2. What kind of schooling do you think you need? Will you take art classes? Will you go to college? How will you learn to be a great artist?

   _____

   _____

   _____

3. What is the work of art that you most want to create? Describe it.

   _____

   _____

   _____

4. What will be the title of your work of art? Why did you choose this title?

   _____

   _____

5. Will you need to travel to do your art? Will you have a studio or other special place to work? Describe how and where you will work.

   _____

   _____

6. How will people describe your art? Write at least four adjectives that describe your style.

   _____

   _____

THE VOYAGEURS

Social Studies

BACKGROUND

This play is set in 1763. Voyageurs were men who were hired by fur trading companies to paddle huge canoes through the Great Lakes region of Canada, trade goods for furs, and then return to Montreal or other posts in Canada. These men were true explorers. Instead of returning home after a voyage, some of them "wintered over" each year (stayed and worked as trappers during the winter) and married Native American women. Their courage, stamina, and good humor made an indelible mark on the history of North America.

WARM-UP ACTIVITY

Use the information sheet on page 100 to introduce students to the voyageurs and the pronunciations of some common French terms. You may also want to use the Internet or library resources to locate images to share with the class. Show pictures of the huge canoes and packs that the voyageurs had to carry. Discuss some of the routes that the explorers and traders took. Then, arrange chairs or desks in a long line to simulate a canoe. Practice

"paddling" with the class. See how long it takes before students start to feel tired or complain. This simple exercise will show students just how difficult it was to be a voyageur—they usually paddled 10- to 16-hour days!

CASTING

The parts in the play are written for readers of different levels, from Level 1 Roles (struggling readers) to Level 4 Roles (advanced readers).

LEVEL 4 ROLES
Narrator #1 and #2   Mrs. Samuel

LEVEL 3 ROLES
Jacques   Pierre   Mr. Samuel
Monsieur Evart   Dawn Sky

LEVEL 2 ROLES
Paul   Running Bear

LEVEL 1 ROLES
Wild Rose   Louis

DISCUSSION

- What do you think the life of a voyageur would be like? Think of some adjectives to describe it.
- Do you think you would have liked being a voyageur? Why or why not?
- What do you think it was like to explore the Great Lakes region of Canada in the 1700s? List some good things and some difficult things about traveling during that time in history.

VOCABULARY TO REVIEW *See page 100 for French pronunciations.*

voyageur	portage	monsieur	pelts	rapids
pemmican	depend (rely)	venison	moccasins	rendezvous

MATH CONNECTION

The voyageur culture is filled with opportunities to create story problems! For example, "If the voyageurs paddled at the rate of 4 miles per hour, and they paddled for 12 hours per day, how long would it take for them to cover 600 miles of waterways?" You can also create math problems about the price of trade goods versus the return on furs.

WRITING CONNECTION

Imagine you are a young voyageur getting ready to start on your first trip across the Great Lakes region of Canada. How do you feel? What do you do to prepare? What advice do the experienced voyageurs offer to you? Write about your preparations as if you are keeping a journal. Then, write at least two more journal entries about exciting adventures during the trip.

COSTUME, PROP, AND SET DESIGN SUGGESTIONS

COSTUMES: *Narrators*—dresses or suits; *Voyageurs*—blue pants, brown loafers, white dress shirts, hooded capes, red hats (winter), bandanas (summer), wigs with ponytails; *Native Americans*—brown pants or dresses, loafers, and ponchos, wigs with long, straight, black hair; *Mrs. Samuel*—collared blouse, long skirt, dark boots, powder to make hair gray, hair in bun; *Mr. Samuel*—white turtleneck, dark vest, suit jacket, dark pants, dress shoes, wig with gray hair in ponytail

PROPS: Oar for each voyageur; two backpacks for each—stuff pillowcases with crumpled newspaper and tie the tops with rope

SET DESIGN: Create a canoe using a large appliance box; artificial Christmas trees or ficus trees placed across back of stage (riverbank); rocks made from papier-mâché and painted gray

SOUND: Play the sound of rushing water while students are paddling. Play the sound of a big splash when voyageur falls into water.

French Pronunciation Guide:

voyageur (ˈvwä-yä-ˈzhər)   monsieur (məs-ˈyə)   rendezvous (ˈrän-dā-vü)

Voyageur is the French word for "traveler." During the 18th and early 19th centuries, voyageurs were men in Canada employed by fur traders and explorers as guides and laborers. Most voyageurs were French or French-Canadian, but there were also those who were European, Russian, African, and Native American. Voyageurs were experts at paddling and maneuvering through treacherous waters from Quebec and Montreal to the regions bordering the Great Lakes.

Why were voyageurs needed?

In the vast area of what is now Canada, there were many Native American tribes. There were also French settlers living in the area that is now Montreal and Quebec. Native Americans were skilled fur trappers, and they were willing to trade their furs for goods, such as knives, beads, wampum, blankets, and other goods. At first, the Native Americans would travel great distances to reach the French settlements. But, over time, ambitious French settlers traveled to meet the Native Americans to assure the best picks of the furs. Furs were in high demand in Europe and Asia, and the settlers could make a good profit trading furs and then selling them overseas. As the settlers began to travel farther and farther to meet the Native Americans, guides and skilled oarsmen became necessary. Therefore, the voyageur profession developed.

What was it like to be a voyageur?

Voyageurs were famous for their strength and endurance. Most of them worked at least 14 hours a day, and they paddled at a rate of almost one stroke per second. Voyageurs traveled in large birch-bark canoes through sometimes dangerous waters and rapids. When the waters became too treacherous, they would portage, which means stop and carry the canoes and packs over land until it was safe to return to the water. When this would happen, each voyageur was expected to carry two 90-pound bundles at once, often over rocky, muddy terrain.

Some voyageurs were known as "pork eaters" because they carried salt pork with them in the canoes for food. They were so busy paddling that there was no time to stop and hunt for fresh meat. Pork eaters would make the journey from Montreal and Quebec to the trading posts at the Great Lakes and then return home for the winter. Other voyageurs, however, would "winter over" in the western areas and continue trapping and trading on their own. Many winterers lived with Native American tribes during the winter months, and some even married Native American women.

 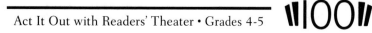

THE VOYAGEURS

CAST

Narrator #1 and #2   Jacques   Wild Rose   Pierre

Dawn Sky   Paul   Running Bear

Monsieur Evart   Louis   Mr. and Mrs. Samuel

SETTING: *Canada, around the Great Lakes and St. Lawrence Seaway. The play opens just outside of Montreal in 1763. The voyageurs are loading their boats to prepare for their journey. It is spring.*

NARRATOR #1: The word voyageur means "traveler" in French. But, the voyageurs we are going to meet were the men who traveled from Montreal to the Great Lakes in the 1700s and 1800s. They were trading for furs.

NARRATOR #2: The voyageurs had to be strong, tough, and smart. We'll learn more about their work. Let's listen. Monsieur Evart is the trading company boss. He is watching the voyageurs load their canoes. You can tell the voyageurs by their red wool caps and deerskin leggings.

MONSIEUR EVART: Pierre, are you sure that you have enough trade goods? Last year, you ran out.

PIERRE: I think so, sir! Let me check: we have cooking pots, knives, guns, and axes.

PAUL: We also have buttons, needles, thread, glass beads, mirrors, and ribbon.

LOUIS: And tea! Don't forget the tea!

MONSIEUR EVART: *(nodding)* That sounds about right. All of those will be traded for furs. Be sure you make good trades. And don't forget: get as many beaver pelts as you can! I cannot keep up with the demand for them from France. Now, where is Jacques?

JACQUES: *(calling)* Here I am, sir!

NARRATOR #1: Jacques is the leader of this group of voyageurs. He will lead them to Grand Portage on Lake Superior. But, he will not come back with them to Montreal. Jacques is a winterer. That means he will stay in the frozen north country all winter long. He will trap for furs and trade them. His wife is there waiting for him.

NARRATOR #2: Pierre, Paul, and Louis are "pork eaters." They get this nickname from the salt pork that they carry with them. They paddle so much that they don't have time to hunt for food. They will paddle all spring and summer to get to the trading posts in the Great Lakes. They will bring as many furs as they can back to Montreal by September. After that, the rivers will be frozen, and they will not be able to travel there again until next spring. Look, the canoe is taking off now.

JACQUES: All right, my brothers! Let's make this a 15-stop day!

VOYAGEURS: Hooray! Paddle hard! We have a long way to go.

NARRATOR #1: The voyageurs would stop to take one break every hour. So, when Jacques said he wanted to make it a "15-stop day," he was talking about paddling for 15 hours!

NARRATOR #2: All summer, the voyageurs will get up at four o'clock in the morning. They will paddle until it is dark. They have hundreds of miles to travel, and they will have to portage their canoe many times.

JACQUES: (calling) There are rapids ahead! Get ready to portage!

LOUIS: (groaning) Can't we just paddle through it?

PIERRE: No, we can't. I know these rapids. They are strong. A friend of mine nearly died here last year.

PAUL: (calling) Get ready to portage!

NARRATOR #1: Portage was one of the worst parts of the journey. It was when they had to carry their canoe across land because it wasn't safe to paddle it. Sometimes there were rapids. Sometimes the water was too shallow. But carrying their canoe and all of their trade goods was no fun!

NARRATOR #2: Just look at that canoe! It's 30 feet long. It's made of wood and birch bark. But, the real weight is the packs. Each pack of trade goods weighs 90 pounds, and each voyageur has to carry two packs—that's 180 pounds! That's in addition to the canoe.

JACQUES: There's a silver dollar for any man who carries more than two packs today! Monsieur Evart has given me money to pay you. Any takers?

PAUL: I will!

PIERRE: He wants the money for his wedding next winter! Ah, Marie has a strong husband-to-be!

LOUIS: I'll just be glad to get our canoe in the water again!

JACQUES: *(calling out)* There's the big, flat rock. That's where we can put the canoe back into the water. Well done, voyageurs!

NARRATOR #1: Many hours later, it is finally time to stop for the night. The voyageurs don't have anything fancy to eat for their supper. Sometimes, they cook dried peas into a soup. Sometimes, they cook cornmeal mush with salt pork.

NARRATOR #2: Later, when they run out of food from the trading company, they will eat pemmican. That's dried buffalo or deer meat. But, they won't have fresh meat until they get to Grand Portage. No time to hunt; just keep paddling!

JACQUES: Pull the canoe into shore, men.

PIERRE: Who wants a game of cat and mouse? How about you, Paul? I'll play you for that silver dollar.

NARRATOR #1: Cat and mouse was the voyageurs' favorite game. Men would stand in the canoe and play tug-of-war. The first person to fall in the water was the loser.

JACQUES: Ah, there goes Paul into the water! He's strong, but his balance is not so good. Too bad, Paul, but don't worry. We'll have plenty of portage before we get to the trading post!

LOUIS: Get some sleep, my brothers. Dawn will be here before you know it.

PAUL: Good night!

NARRATOR #2: These voyageurs are French Canadian, and most of them were. But, there are records that show there were some British, African, and Russian voyageurs, too. And, there were Native Americans who worked with the voyageurs. Most of them were from the Iroquois and Ottawa nations. Some voyageurs, especially the winterers, married Native American women. Jacques's wife is a Native American woman.

JACQUES: (calling out) Look, it's Running Bear, my brother-in-law! How good to see you. What are you doing here, so far from Grand Portage?

RUNNING BEAR: I was helping a friend take some supplies to his summer camp. I will help paddle if you want me to.

PAUL: You will be most welcome!

LOUIS: Yes, we can always use the help. Welcome, Running Bear!

JACQUES: How is my wife, Wild Rose? Has your sister been well these past months that I've been gone?

RUNNING BEAR: She is well. She will be very happy to see you. She has been making a rabbit-fur quilt for your cabin.

PAUL: What is that?

JACQUES: It's a rabbit-fur robe with cloth on both sides to hold in the heat. It's very warm—much better than a wool blanket. Wild Rose is a great seamstress.

NARRATOR #1: It was very common during the 1700s for French Canadians to have Native American wives. The voyageurs who wintered over in the harsh north country depended on the help of the Native Americans for many things.

NARRATOR #2: And later, the Native Americans grew to depend on the voyageurs' trade goods. Some chiefs encouraged the trade. Some felt it was a bad idea to trade too much with the white men. But, look! Now, the voyageurs have finally made it to their trading post. Mr. and Mrs. Samuel have walked down to the dock to greet them.

MRS. SAMUEL: Jacques! It's good to see you! Welcome home. And welcome to you, brave voyageurs. I will make a meal for you tonight.

LOUIS: What will you make for us, madame?

MRS. SAMUEL: *(smiling)* How does venison stew sound to you?

PIERRE: After weeks of cornmeal mush, it sounds like the best meal I can possibly imagine!

PAUL: Yes, indeed!

MR. SAMUEL: Welcome, all! Have you brought all of the trade goods that Monsieur Evart promised? I have his list.

JACQUES: Yes, sir. You and I can check it together after our supper. But right now, I would like to see my wife. I have missed her! Is she here?

MR. SAMUEL: I think she is in the kitchen. She's been staying here with us for a few days, waiting for you. *(calling)* Wild Rose!

WILD ROSE: *(calling out)* Jacques! It is you! You are here at last!

NARRATOR #1: The voyageurs who were married had to leave their families for months at a time. That's why Wild Rose always looked forward to winter. She and Jacques would be together the whole winter while he trapped furs. She would help him clean the pelts for trading. And, she would make sure they had enough food to get through the winter.

NARRATOR #2: The winters were long in this area. The first snows would start in September or October. The smaller rivers would not thaw until May. But winter was the best time to trap because the animals had heavy winter fur.

MR. SAMUEL: I have run out of everything I had to trade. But now that you've arrived, the trading can begin again.

RUNNING BEAR: My wife badly needs a new cooking pot. Here she is now. Dawn Sky, Jacques is back with us!

DAWN SKY: Welcome home, my husband. And welcome, my brother-in-law Jacques! I hope you have some beads and thread in those packs. I have to make a new pair of moccasins for our little one.

PAUL: You will find everything you want and need here, Dawn Sky. It's trading time again.

NARRATOR #1: Native Americans would come to the trading post at Grand Portage in the coming weeks with all of the furs they had trapped the winter before. They would trade them for things that they needed and wanted—knives and guns to help them hunt, needles and thread to help them make clothing, and other things for their homes and families.

NARRATOR #2: At the end of the summer, there would be a big rendezvous. That was a big gathering that was like a trading party and going-away party all at once. The trappers would bring the last of their furs. The voyageurs who weren't winterers would gather to travel back to Montreal together. There would be games and songs and big meals. Then, it was time to say good-bye.

JACQUES: Farewell, brave voyageurs! Travel safely!

DAWN SKY: We will see you next spring!

LOUIS: Farewell!

MR. SAMUEL: It feels colder tonight.

MRS. SAMUEL: *(smiling)* It's the start of winter, my dear.

WILD ROSE: Yes! Winter—the best part of the year.

JACQUES: Let's go home, Wild Rose!

COMPREHENSION QUESTIONS

Match the words to their meanings. Write the letters in the blanks.

_____ 1. moccasins a. French for "traveler"

_____ 2. monsieur b. soft leather shoes

_____ 3. pelts c. a big gathering

_____ 4. rendezvous d. the fur and skins of animals

_____ 5. portage e. to carry a canoe across the land

_____ 6. voyageur f. French for "sir"

Write a short answer.

7. What was Jacques' job with the fur trading company?

_____

8. List four things that the voyageurs carried with them as trade goods.

_____

_____

9. Explain the difference between a "winterer" and a "pork eater."

_____

_____

_____

10. List three things that would be difficult on a voyageur's trip across the Great Lakes. What possible dangers were there?

_____

_____

_____

DATE _____

COMPREHENSION ACTIVITY

Imagine you have been offered a job as a voyageur. In the chart, write pros (positive things) and cons (negative things) about the new job. The first one is done for you.

PROS (POSITIVE THINGS)	CONS (NEGATIVE THINGS)
1. I would only have to work for six months of the year!	1. I would have to endure long hours of paddling through sometimes dangerous waters.
2.	2.
3.	3.
4.	4.
5.	5.
6.	6.

7. Based on what you've written in your chart, would you take the job? Why or why not?

_____

_____

Page 19

1. d
2. c
3. a
4. He is nervous because he is struggling in social studies, and he doesn't want to disappoint his dad.
5. He was too scared and didn't really get a chance to explain what happened.
6. No. Her feelings were hurt because she wasn't invited to the party, and she took it out on Nikki.

Page 20

Answers will vary.

Page 31

1. b
2. a
3. c

Answers for 4–13 will vary but may include:

4. pretty
5. concerned
6. strong
7. boiling
8. student
9. shiny
10. bright
11. funny
12. cloudy
13. slow

Page 32

Answers will vary.

Page 44

1. b
2. c
3. a
4. d
5. c

Page 44 (continued)

6. She wanted Cinderella to be more ladylike and go to dance classes.
7. She had a frilly, white dress and black patent-leather shoes.

Page 45

Compare and contrast answers will vary, but may include:

Stepmothers: compare–both are stepmothers, both are in charge of Cinderella; contrast–the stepmother in the play is nice, she lets Cinderella do what she wants to do

Stepsisters: compare–all are stepsisters, all want to go to the ball; contrast–the stepsisters in the play are friendly to Cinderella, they want her to go to the ball

Prince Charming and Brendan: compare–both find a lost shoe, both want to find Cinderella; contrast–Brendan is not a prince, he wants her to be on the baseball team

Cinderellas: compare–both are unhappy at the beginning of the story, both have a fairy godparent; contrast–Cinderella in the play wants to play sports, she doesn't want to wear a pretty dress

Answers to 1–2 will vary.

Page 56

1. They are trying to demolish an old office building that represents the number 17,892.
2. They successfully bring down the building and receive their next job assignment.
3. NO
4. c
5. a
6. b
7. b
8. a

Page 57

Answers will vary. Drawings should correspond to answers given for 1–4.

Page 70
1. b
2. c
3. a
4. d
5. b
6. Lee didn't come to camp on the last day, so he never got to tell Jamal about the treasure hunt.
7. Answers will vary but may include: thoughtful (Lee gave Jamal something special because he knew Jamal liked it), creative (Lee made up the treasure hunt), a good friend (Jamal says this, and it is evident in the letter Lee wrote)

Page 71

5, 4, 1, 6, 7, 2, 3

Drawings will vary but should match the directions.

Page 83
1. d
2. b
3. b
4. The soldiers wanted souvenirs of the surrender.
5. General Grant and General Lee
6. b
7. c

Page 84

Answers will vary.

Page 96
1. b
2. e
3. d

Page 96 (continued)
4. c
5. a
6. f

Answers to 7–10 will vary but may include:
7. George did everything he ever wanted to do during his life.
8. His parents were worried because they thought painting and traveling would be bad for his health.
9. Italy, Lackawanna Valley, Niagara Falls, Florida, California
10. A field of tree stumps in the foreground; a roundhouse, train tracks, and two trains in the distance

Page 97

Answers will vary.

Page 109
1. b
2. f
3. d
4. c
5. e
6. a
7. Jacques is the leader of the group of voyageurs.
8. Answers will vary but may include: cooking pots, knives, guns, glass beads, ribbons, thread, buttons
9. A "winterer" didn't return to Montreal after trading for furs; instead, he "wintered over" and trapped furs. A "pork eater" returned to Montreal for the winter.
10. Answers will vary.

Page 110

Answers will vary.